CHRIST ASCENDED

A Study in the Significance of the Ascension of Jesus Christ

Brian K. Donne M.A.

CHRIST ASCENDED

A Study in
The Significance of the Ascension of Jesus Christ
in
The New Testament

EXETER
THE PATERNOSTER PRESS

AUSTRALIA
Bookhouse Australia Ltd.,
P.O. Box 115, Flemington Markets,
N.S.W. 2129.

SOUTH AFRICA
Oxford University Press,
P.O. Box 1141, Cape Town.

British Library Cataloguing in Publication Data

Donne, B.K.
Christ ascended.
1. Jesus Christ—Ascension
I. Title
233.9'7 BT500

ISBN 0-85364-336-9

Photoset in Great Britain by
Photo-Graphics, Honiton, Devon
and printed for The Paternoster Press,
Paternoster House, 3 Mount Radford Crescent, Exeter, Devon
by A. Wheaton & Co. Ltd, Exeter

Contents

Preface

During my course as a theological student in Cheshunt College, Cambridge, there came into my possession a copy of *The Appearances of Our Lord after the Passion* by Dr. H.B. Swete, who was Regius Professor of Divinity in Cambridge at the time of the publication of that book in 1907 (it was reprinted in 1908 (twice), 1910, 1912, 1915). That book proved to be a source of abiding interest and continuing inspiration, and the words of Professor Swete in the Foreword have become increasingly important for me, especially since undertaking the study of the Ascension in recent years. He wrote, "Few things are more important than that Christian people should learn to realize the fact of our Lord's risen and ascended life, and its relation to their own lives and hopes". This essay is an attempt, in some small way, to renew interest in a subject of vital importance in our present disorganised and uncertain age, and, at the same time, to seek to uphold what St. Augustine so boldly stated in the fifth century when he said, "This is that festival which confirms the grace of all the festivals together, without which the profitableness of every festival would have perished". (Sermo 53.4 – Coll. Selec. SS Ecclesiae Patrum, ed. D.A.B. Caillau, 131B, 1842, p. 278, quoted by Dr. J.G. Davies in *He Ascended into Heaven*, Bampton Lectures, 1958, p. 170). If therefore, the attempt here to show the Ascension as having the greatest possible significance in holding together the cardinal doctrines of the Christian faith, and in expressing the communication of the life of the glorified Christ to his people is successful, then the aim of the present writer, in his calling as a minister as he seeks to proclaim the

Crucified, Risen and Ascended Saviour and Lord, will have been further pursued through the medium of the written as well as the spoken word.

My indebtedness to many sources is clearly evident, and I welcome the opportunity of making reference to particular means of help in this study. As far as I am aware, all the major works in English of the Ascension are now out of print, and were it not for the invaluable supply of these and related works in the Dr. Williams's Library, the writing of this book would have been virtually impossible. I am most grateful to the Library Staff for so readily making available such books as have been requested, always with the greatest efficiency and courtesy.

In recent years, many theological writings by authors on the Continent have been translated into English, copies of which are among the fine collection of volumes in the Bristol Baptist College Library. The Principal of the College, the Rev. L.G. Champion, B.A., B.D., D.Th., now Principal-Emeritus, not only generously offered me the facilities of the Library, but also very kindly agreed to supervise my work in its later stages. His counsel was more than ever appreciated in that, during the twelve months when I was attending the College Library, Dr. Champion held the demanding office of Moderator of the National Free Church Federal Council. Moreover, as a guest of the College for lunch on the occasion of my weekly visits to the Library, I had valuable contacts with both Staff and Students which were much appreciated.

Two sources of financial assistance were offered to me while undertaking this research. The late Rev. A.R. Vine, M.A., B.Sc., D.D., who was then the General Secretary of the Free Church Federal Council and Clerk to the Trustees of the Brand Charitable Trust, made it possible for me to receive pecuniary aid, available under the terms of that Trust to ministers proceeding to further academical studies while in the pastorate. I remember with gratitude this kindness of Dr. Vine, and express my thanks to the Trustees for their generous assistance in this way. When it became necessary for me to travel each week to Bristol, Dr. Champion mentioned the Bristol Baptist Fund as a probable source of help towards travelling expenses, and I remain indebted to the Committee of that Fund for the provision of a grant for that purpose.

An abridged version of this book was published in the *Scottish Journal of Theology*, Volume 30 No. 6 (1977), pp. 555–568 by the Scottish Academic Press Limited, and to Mr. Douglas Grant, F.R.S.E., the Managing Director, I owe my very real thanks for his kindly giving me permission to make available in more detail, the contents of that earlier publication.

Before the acceptance of this work for publication, there occurred the sudden and unexpected death at his home in Richmond of the Rev. A. Marcus Ward, M.A., D.D., who, after a missionary teaching career in Bangalore, India, became lecturer in New Testament studies at Richmond College, Divinity School, University of London, and subsequently held a similar position on the staff of Heythrop College in London University. It is with the greatest pleasure that I recall our discussions, both personally and through considerable correspondence on a subject in which he also was deeply interested. He had read the typescript of this work to which he gave his unequivocal support, and gave much encouragement as he continued to share my hope of the longer text being published.

With the many and varied commitments of the ministry, any research obviously makes considerable demands upon one's time, and I am indeed appreciative of the help given by my wife Margaret, and my family, for their understanding and encouragement which has made possible the writing of this book.

TROWBRIDGE, BRIAN K. DONNE.
WILTSHIRE.

Abbreviations

C.Q.R.	Church Quarterly Review
ET.	English Translation
Exp.T.	Expository Times
J.B.L.	Journal of Biblical Literature
J.T.S.	Journal of Theological Studies
N.E.B.	New English Bible.
S.B.T.	Studies in Biblical Theology
S.J.T.	Scottish Journal of Theology
S.N.T.S.	Studorium Novi Testamenti Societas

The Biblical Text used throughout, except where otherwise stated is the Revised Standard Version, Old Testament Section, 1952 and New Testament Section, 1946.

Introduction

Of all the festivals in the Christian year, the Ascension receives the least attention of any, and, falling as it does, always on a Thursday, the fortieth day after Easter Sunday, it is frequently passed by unnoticed, or, if it is observed at all, is not likely to generate enthusiasm to any extent among the vast majority of worshippers.[1] This is understandable for two main reasons. After the glory of Easter, with its triumph of victory, the parting of the Risen Lord from his disciples does suggest something of an anti-climax on a *prima facie* level for most people, and the apparent suggetion of an upward levitation in a post-Copernican, space-age, which measures distances in terms of 'light years', seems so remote and even so ludicrous[2] as to warrant instant dismissal from the mind. Again, the narrative of the Ascension is found only in the Lucan writings, and since both the Third Gospel and the Acts of the Apostles are later than the Pauline writings (where Resurrection and Exaltation are frequently brought together as a single theme), it is often assumed that the Ascension is a purely Lucan concept to describe the termination of the post-Resurrection appearances. Further, the linking of Paul's conversion experience on the Damascus Road with the post-Resurrection appearances[3] has been seen as proof that no separate Ascension event, as such, occurred. The general acceptance until recently of the observance of the Ascension as a separate festival from the fourth century onwards, before which it has been thought to have been celebrated as a part of the Easter event,[4] has further contributed to the idea that Resurrection and Ascension belong inseparably together, and that if any distinction exists at all, it is solely one of theology and not of chronology. The German scholar, A. von Harnack,[5] towards the end of the last century formulated his views on these lines which have largely influenced Biblical scholarship for more than half a century. H.B. Swete[6] made a spirited reply to Harnack's position, and since his writings in the early part of this century, most of the published work has been in the form of articles in theological journals and commentaries, though Professor J.G. Davies' Bampton Lectures, He Ascended into Heaven,[7] were devoted to the subject, and a few years afterwards, Professor U.E. Simon published, The Ascent to Heaven.[8] Much more recently, Professor T.F. Torrance published, Space, time and resurrection,[9] of which the greater part of the second half deals directly with the Ascension. It is worthy of note that a significant number of contemporary authors outside the British Isles, in works of considerable importance which have been translated into English, accept the Ascension narrative as it appears both in the Third Gospel and in the Acts of the Apostles, thereby showing their recognition of Luke as the 'Father of Church History'[10].

Before examining the text in detail, and the problems which arise from it, we must first enquire as to how far the Ascension is integral to the New Testament as a whole. If the Resurrection of Jesus Christ is seen to be the focal point of the New Testament, is anything more needed?[11] If the "Resurrection of Jesus meant simultaneously his exaltation",[12] and the whole of the New Testament is written from the standpoint of the Exalted Lord,[13] does not the Ascension then become superfluous?

We best answer this by considering how the New Testament regards the Resurrection of Christ. As Professor L. Hodgson put the matter, "all Christians...would be agreed that our Lord's life did not end on Calvary, that in some way He now lives on as the unseen Lord and Master of us all. But then there arises a dispute between those who speak of a 'bodily' and those who speak of a 'purely spiritual' Resurrection".[14] Yet it has to be admitted that to relegate the Resurrection to a place entirely outside the sphere of history, would be contrary to the Gospel narratives as we have them, and would still leave unanswered the question as to how it became known that the post-Resurrection appearances had then come to an end. That the Risen Christ was seen is the undoubted teaching of the Gospels, and the Ascension becomes a necessity to indicate that he would no longer appear in that way until the Parousia. And if we are going to accept the evidence of the Gospels for the Empty Tomb as "a constant feature of the Gospel witness",[15] which together with the appearances constitute the foundation for belief in the Resurrection of Jesus, then the Ascension must have a place in history, although only Luke records it as such in narrative form. Furthermore, in our analysis of other relevant New Testament passages, it will be shown that references to the Ascension are there by inference, and sometimes stated directly, thereby revealing the theological significance of the Ascension of our Lord throughout the New Testament.

PART ONE

Analysis of Relevant New Testament Passages

CHAPTER ONE

The Lucan Writings

THE GOSPEL OF ST. LUKE

The first narrative account of the Ascension occurs in St. Luke 24:50–53 with the Risen Christ leading his disciples out as far as Bethany, lifting up his hands, blessing them, and being parted from them. As the story stands, it gives the impression that the parting took place on the evening of Easter Day. Yet, even if this was the case (the reference in Acts 1:3 to the forty days interval being disregarded), and the separation was only a matter of hours, instead of nearly six weeks, the description of the event would clearly indicate a definite and final taking of leave of his disciples by Jesus, quite separate from the Resurrection.

The text continues in certain versions in verse 51b, "and was carried up into heaven", but this is omitted in various manuscripts (ℵD a b e ff^2 j l (sy^s)). In a full examination of this verse, C. S. C. Williams believes that since the Ascension formed part of the early proclamation of the Good News, mention should be expected of it in at least one of the written Gospels. As he says, "If the Western omission is correct, there is no reference at all to the Ascension in the original text of the Gospels, Mark XVI:19 being part of the unauthentic Longer Ending. It is not improbable that the words were penned by St. Luke, and that the words were omitted intentionally from the 'Western' text on the ground that they could be taken to imply that Jesus' Ascension occurred on the very day of His Resurrection, which would conflict with the account in Acts 1:3f, according to which Christ ascended forty days after His Resurrection".[1]

At this stage in our discussion, it would be appropriate to consider other reasons which are thought to have led to the omission of the words of verse 51b.[2]

One reason which seems fairly obvious is that the omission makes for smoother continuity between the narrative in the Gospel and the author's second volume, the Acts of the Apostles, in which Luke refers in the opening verses to "all that Jesus began to do and teach, until the day when he was taken up"; and this would appear to be supported by the view that Luke 9:51, where *analēmpseōs*[3] begins the final section of the Gospel– "When the days drew near for him to be received up, he set his face to go to Jerusalem" – leading to his assumption.

Another view is that Luke/Acts formed a single volume which was later separated into two parts, and verse 51b was inserted to make a complete ending to the first part. A. N. Wilder[4] thinks the true text probably included "and was carried up into heaven", but that its omission in the Western Text is due, both to a desire to minimize the difficulty of the forty days interval, and to note that the whole of Luke 24:50–53 was added as a summary of Acts 1:1–11 when the works were separated. Similarly, J.M. Creed believes that when the two manuscripts were divided, "a more emphatic conclusion to the Gospel was felt desirable, and the same editor's hand which supplemented the account of the Lord's Supper from St. Paul and harmonized the Resurrection narratives with those of the other Gospels, has also amplified the text of these last verses to include a direct statement of the Ascension into heaven".[5]

Still further, there are those who think that Luke received information later concerning the forty days interval between the Resurrection and the Ascension which he did not correct in his earlier account, since he did not know of the fact until he came to write the opening verses of Acts.[6]

While J. H. Ropes believes that reference to the Ascension is absent from both Luke 24:51 and Acts 1:2, "until the day when he was taken up", he rejects the view that the original 'B' text was deliberately mutilated in order to harmonize the two accounts as the motive would be insufficient, and fails to explain the excision of *anelēmphthē* in Acts 1:2.[7]

The climate of opinion in more recent years, most noticeably among writers on the Continent, has been to accept the full text as being original.[8] Haenchen may be cited in this connection when he says, "As has been seen even more clearly in recent years, the ascension actually possesses a somewhat different meaning at the conclusion of Luke than at the beginning of Acts: it triumphantly closes the existence of the Lord on earth. In the context of Acts, on the other hand, it links the instruction of the disciples by the risen Lord – and thus the Church's instruction by him – with the further history of the Christian proclamation and the growing congregation. The correction which the 'Western' text achieves by deleting *kai anephereto eis ton ouranon*, has only perceived the conflict, but has not grasped the freedom with which Luke, by the rise of two different traditions, had expressed the different aspects of the ascension".[9]

Moreover, as Haenchen points out, the fact of leading the disciples to Bethany in itself is an indication of anticipated parting from them, and "represents the most fitting conclusion to the gospel from the literary point of view".[10]

Again, the *Proskunēsantes auton* in verse 52, omitted in D it sy^{cs}, has been excluded because of the failure to recognise that here was the moment of adoration before One who, in parting from them, lifted up his hands in blessing and, "was carried up into heaven". Here we have a liturgical presentation of the ascending Christ as Luke "moulds the last Christophany into a splendid vision of Christ as a 'blessing priest'...Luke gives at the end of his Gospel a 'doxological' interpretation of the Ascension".[11] Certainly, it would seem that the narrative of Luke 24:50–53 is expanded and developed in the Acts of the Apostles as indicated by the reference back in chapter 1:1. As D. P. Fuller says, "Thus the three accounts of the ascension in Luke 24.50–Acts 1.9 are not the result of clumsy editing, for each has its distinctive function. Luke 24.51 provides the climax to the Gospel of Luke. Acts 1.2 reiterates this climax so that the reader will not forget the point of the Gospel while proceeding with the Acts. Acts 1.9–11 sets forth the ascension as terminating the resurrection appearances so they can function as the basis of what follows".[12] C. F. Evans feels that the ending of Luke 24.51 is "as jejune a description as possible of the ascension, and hardly forms a climax to a process which Luke had already described in 9.51 as an analēmpsis or assumption[13]," and that Acts 1:9–11 forms a better climax. But since the process has been set in motion in the final section of the Gospel at 9.51 leading to the Ascension, (of which the readers are reminded in acts 1:2), the process continues in the ministry of the Ascending Christ in Acts 1:9–11. This is anticipated here in the coming of the Spirit at Pentecost[14] whereby the Church is born, and the intercessory ministry of Christ in heaven, all of which are set in motion by the historical account of the Ascension event. What Hastings Rashdall said in another connection has relevance here, "... it does not seem to me possible to recognise the claim of any historical religion to be final and ultimate, unless it include within itself a principle of development"[15]. The Ascension marks the final and ultimate point of the revelation of God in Christ Incarnate in this world, and, at the same time, it inaugurates the developing process of the Father's purpose "as a plan for the fullness of time, to unite all things in him, things in heaven and things on earth" (Eph. 1:10). The Gospel account, which is doxological, appears to anticipate this process as the author portrays the Ascending Christ blessing his disciples beyond the bounds of the temple, thereby preparing them to go out into the world as his witnesses.[16] Yet they return to Jerusalem with great joy, and are continually in the temple blessing God (Luke 24:52–53), as they learn of new relationships with his unseen presence, in readiness for being his "witnesses in Jerusalem and in all Judea and Samaria and to the end of the earth" (Acts 1:8). The joyful return to Jerusalem indicated that here was no ordinary parting,[17] but one accompanied by his blessing, the undoubted assurance of his abiding presence always in time and for eternity.

THE ACTS OF THE APOSTLES

The continuity between the Third Gospel and the Acts of the Apostles is indicated in the opening verse of the latter which is addressed to Theophilus, and the reference back to his being "taken up" (*anelēmphthē*) in the next verse. The third verse would seem to be by way of explanation that what is being referred to at the conclusion of the Gospel and in Acts 1:2, took place after an interval of forty days, a Biblical round number, which here would appear to be intended literally.[18] Attempts to delete it create more problems than they seek to solve, since "forty" always indicates a definite interval of time,[19] and its usage here corrects any suggestion which may have previously been given of Resurrection and Ascension as being one event on the same occasion. Indeed, acceptance of the forty days' interval allows time for the disciples to return to Galilee following the Passover Festival in a crowded Jerusalem, and then return to the Holy City for Pentecost in ample time for another busy festival occasion.[20]

It is in the nature of the case that the historical accounts of Acts 1:1–11 is not as straightforward as might have been expected, and indeed, "Acts 1.1–5 is an extraordinary sentence of which it is impossible to establish either the syntax or the translation of the text as usually printed...it is overloaded with participles, some of which are awkardly connected with verbs (e.g. vv. 2 and 4), and at v.5, it changes abruptly from indirect to direct speech".[21] Moreover, it opens with a *men* clause, but the expected *de* clause to follow does not appear, though as Haenchen observes, this is a frequent feature in Acts, and the change from indirect to direct speech in Acts is used by Luke in the interests of flexibility.[22] Nevertheless, there is a concise and unmistakable account of the Ascension in 1:9–11, and to Luke, it is of the utmost importance that the Risen Christ who had been with his disciples during the forty days, should now ascend to the Father, and the new age of the Church begin.[23] van Stempvoort expresses it in this way when he says "the Church cannnot forever remain in the attitude of proskunenis and eulogia...Acts must follow the Gospel and after Easter, the history of a 'collectivism', the Church began. Luke was the first to begin the great task of writing that new history. That he has done it brilliantly may be seen in his second version of the Ascension in Acts".[24]

Probably the greatest stumbling-block to the modern mind is the literal idea of an ascension into the spiritual sphere. It might be asked if such a portrayal of the event is not too infantile in a modern scientific age which talks and thinks in terms of light years and explores outer space. Let it be said in reply that even the most profound interpretation of the Ascension can never explain all that such an event means in technical terminology, and that, in any case, the *meaning* of the Ascension is of far greater importance than the manner of our Lord's final departure from this world. As Professor Moule reminds us, "he (Luke) clearly believed that something significant did 'happen' ... it is described as a decisive and deliberate withdrawal from sight, to be distinguished from the mere 'disappearance' in the Emmaus story (*aphanatos egeneto ap'autōn*)...in short, there seems to be no intrinsic reason for not accepting the Ascension as something (of course, we cannot define precisely what) which vividly and ocularly conveyed these convictions (the closing of a chapter and the opening of a new chapter) to the disciples".[25] Clearly Luke used the best description available to express the event as given to him by first-hand witnesses of the occasion.

The Risen Christ appeared in a Body of Glory, and was as ready to go to the Father on Easter Day as he was at the conclusion of the forty day period.[26] Where he was during this interval can only be left to conjecture, but there does not seem to be sufficient Scriptural evidence to suggest that each appearance was a descent from heaven of a Lord who had ascended to heaven the moment he was raised from death.[27] For while during the forty days he came suddenly and departed as suddenly without warning, with these post-resurrection appearances bearing a distinctive characteristic from all subsequent revelations after the Ascension[28], there *is* reason to believe that the Risen Christ was with them, sharing things concerning the Kingdom of God, and "eating with them" (Acts 1:4), this being the alternative to "staying with them",[29] on more occasions than the ten recorded in the New Testament, when he appeared to the disciples. It could well be that the process of his transformation was completed during this period as Barclay hints when he draws attention to the use of the present tense of the verb (*anabainō*) "I am ascending"[30] (John 20:17), and while this cannot be substantiated in any definite way, it could be that, since as we shall show later, our spiritual ascension depends upon his bodily Ascension, yet for him, a process which was completed in that period, anticipated the process which those who are in Christ will experience fully and finally in the heavenly realm.[31]

What is clear, however, is that the Ascension was necessary for the disciples to realize that this was the last occasion when he would manifest himself visibly until the Parousia. For "there must have been...some manifestation of the Risen Christ which they recognised as the last of a series, and which in some respects was unlike those which preceded it...those who do not admit the narrative based on historical event are under the necessity of explaining how the disciples, whose only strength was in the conviction of the nearness of their Risen Master, should have been led to imagine that the gracious Epiphanies of His presence had suddenly come to an end".[32]

Writing an account some twenty years after the event, and selecting his material in accordance with his intended purpose, Luke, in using sources which are available, believes that he is recording events as they actually happened, of which the Ascension is one as seen by eye-witnesses.[33] And the Ascension as it is described, lays emphasis upon the fact that his going "into *heaven*", (the phrase occurs four times "like a refrain" in the Acts narrative (Acts 1:2, 9, 10, 11)[34] and once in the Gospel narrative) is visibly seen by the Twelve.[35] The narrative is of a movement upwards which is the only way of describing it in order to convey the desired impression of his entry into the eternal sphere.[36] The transformed and glorified Lord could not forever remain on earth and his "end had to come in *glorification* and not in *dissolution*".[37] van Stempvoort says that "verse 9 gives in *eperthē* (elevatus est) the concrete description of an event; *epairō* has verticality...Dutch translations unanimously give 'a cloud took him away from their eyes' or 'a cloud withdrew him from their eyes'. But in the first instance, the verb does *not* mean 'withdraw' or 'take away', but '*to take up*' (and carry away)... translations 'withdraw from', 'hide from', 'take away', are mystical interpretations. But Luke realistically stresses final separation – 'a cloud took him up by getting under him (and so took him) out of their sight! If we follow the normal meaning of *hupolambanō* in this way, the cloud is not a fog cloud hiding a mystery, but a royal chariot showing the reality of the disappearance of Christ"[38]

In this connection, it is important to observe that the word "to rise" from the dead (*egeirein*), and the world "to resurrect" (*anistēmi*) never refer to anything more than the mere recall from death, back to earth, whereas *anabainō* is always concerned with a rising upwards, and, as applied to our Lord's Ascension, means of necessity his rising upwards *from* the earth, as distinct from his being brought back to life *on* earth.[39]

Since it is emphasised that the disciples witnessed visibly this rising of the ascending Lord, in so far that meaning "to look intently", "to gaze", even "to stare", shows Luke's realism,[40] it is difficult to understand why Dr. Ramsey says that no one actually saw the Ascension happen, in the same way that no one saw the Resurrection happen.[41] For while the latter statement is perfectly true, the very opposite would seem to be the case where the Ascension is concerned, and interestingly, Ramsey cites J. H. Bernard that the Ascension was the last of a series given to convince the disciples that the Risen Lord would no longer be seen by them in that way.[42] The skyward looking is not forbidden,[43] and, as Professor Bruce says, "We need not be alarmed by the ascension story being bound up with pre-Copernican conception of the universe, and that therefore, it is obsolete. Anyone appearing to leave the earth's surface must appear to spectators to be ascending, and so, when the cloud enveloped the visible form of the Lord, His disciples stood 'looking stedfastly into heaven as He went".[44] In the final analysis, it is surely no more difficult to accept the *idea* of the Ascension than it is to accept the concept of Resurrection or the fact of the Incarnation.[45] The Ascension has nothing whatever to do with Ptolemaic astronomy in terms of a journey from earth to heaven, for the post-resurrection appearances demonstrate that the boundaries of space and time are limitations which, for the Risen Christ, can no longer exist.[46]

CONCLUSION

Our survey of the Lucan narratives of the Ascension reveals that there are two accounts of the one event; they do not coincide in every detail because they are different in purpose as we have seen, but they do clearly indicate a definite and final parting which is distinct from the Resurrection. As Stauffer says, "In the account of the Ascension in primitive Christianity, many different motifs from different traditions and ways of presentation can be found alongside each other modified. It is easy enough to see that the essential thing is not how the Ascension took place but that it occurred!".[47] Further confirmation of this is to be found in Haenchen who writes "Here we must remind ourselves that Luke does not set as much store as we upon consistency in the story...to Luke, it is of the utmost importance that Acts should begin, not with the disciples left to their own devices, but with the Lord, who visits and instructs them forty days more ... this Ascension after forty days is however, suitable only for Acts, not for the end of Luke. There the normal version is appropriate, according to which Jesus took his leave on the night of Easter Sunday. And, of course, in ceremonial fashion: hence the gesture of benediction, which makes a peculiarly deep impression on the reader because of its very singularity...it is thus by no means necessary to assume Luke only heard about the forty days after his first book had appeared".[48]

With Luke's claim to be self-confessed narrator of the New Testament as he states in the opening words of his Gospel, we may accept the reference to the forty days as being, not the work of an interpolator, but the genuine dating of one who has "undertaken to compile a narrative of the things which have been accomplished among us just as they were delivered to us by those who from the beginning were eye-witnesses ... it seemed ... good...having followed all things closely for some time past to write an orderly account for you...that you may know the truth concerning the things of which you have been informed" (St. Luke 1:1–4).[49] Although, as Moule says, he "would be the last to dogmatise about the forty days, yet a better case may be made than is sometimes imagined for 'dating' the event in the manner indicated in the opening verses of the Acts"[50].

CHAPTER TWO

Other New Testament Writings

THE GOSPEL OF ST. MATTHEW

The first Gospel, after recounting the Resurrection scene, moves quickly from Jerusalem to Galilee, and the emphasis lies upon the Risen Christ being met and seen there. The message is given by the angel at the Empty Tomb in Jerusalem, "He is not here; for he has risen, as he said...then go quickly and tell his disciples that he has risen from the dead, and behold, he is going before you to Galilee; there you will see him. Lo, I have told you" (St. Matthew 28:6f). The final scene depicts the eleven disciples meeting the Risen Christ in Galilee on a mountain to which Jesus had directed them, the giving of the Great Commission, and the promise of his abiding presence "to the close of the age" (St. Matthew 28:16f).

Matthew therefore, has post-resurrection appearances in both Jerusalem and Galilee,[1] since as soon as the women leave the tomb, they encounter the Risen Christ (28:9), and it is now he who confirms the earlier message of the angel when he says, "Go and tell my brethren to go to Galilee, and there they will see me" (28:10). It is possible that the reference in 1 Corinthians 15:6[2] to "more than five hundred brethren at one time", may refer to this occasion, since the fact that "some doubted" (28:17) could, it has been suggested, mean that the company comprised more than the *eleven* disciples. Although the words of the Risen Christ in v.19, "Go...and make disciples of all nations" bear a similarity to the words of St. Luke 24:47 "that repentance and forgiveness of sins should be preached in his name to all nations, beginning from Jerusalem", and to those of Acts 1:8, "you shall be my witnesses in Jerusalem and in Judea and Samaria and to the end of the earth", it is not possible to identify the Matthean account with that of Luke-Acts, since the location is different,[3] but it may well be that in Galilee, the Risen Christ is preparing his disciples for the time when they will again be in Jerusalem for Pentecost when, the Holy Spirit having been received, (as is similarly promised in the Luke-Acts account), they will be empowered to put into operation the command of the Risen Christ.[4] As Swete says, "The first Gospel cannot fairly be said to omit the Ascension, for it does not carry the reader so far, stopping short with the meeting in Galilee"[5], and yet, already he has "all authority in heaven and on earth" (28:18) by reason of his having been raised up from the dead. And it is by that same power he will be taken up into heaven (cf: Acts 2:24–36), as it is that he will fulfil his promise to be with his followers all the days, though no longer seen ocularly as he was during the forty days. The appearance in Galilee cannot, therefore, be post-Ascension, only post-Resurrection, unless we accept one or other of two alternatives, namely, that each post-Resurrection appearance was also post-Ascension[6], or that the post-Resurrection appearances were spiritual visions[7], and therefore, were in no way objective. Neither of these alternatives is implied in the Luke/Acts accounts of the Ascension, and the Matthean version of his final meeting with the eleven disciples must be seen to anticipate rather than to follow the Ascension. At some stage, he must have been no longer seen by them, but his departure is unrecorded by the author of the first Gospel.

THE GOSPEL OF ST. MARK

The earliest in time of the four Gospels to have been written is generally thought to have concluded at 16:8 "for they were afraid" with the last twelve verses having been added at a later date. This Longer Ending is a summary account of the Lucan material, and there is a "lack of report in the oldest tradition (אB k sy^{sin} and testimony of Eusebius and Hieronymus), and also a divergent character of text in respect of the other Gospels".[8]

The abrupt ending *ephobounto gar* (16:8) suggests that the original Longer Ending may have been lost or intentionally removed. If the latter were the reaason, it would be on account of Mark 14:28 and 16:7 referring to the Risen Christ being seen in Galilee, and, since the Lucan express command was for the disciples to stay in Jerusalem (Acts 1:4), it would mean that to allow the Longer Ending to remain would reveal a disobedience and a discrepancy when the two were placed side by side. One way to obviate this would be to remove it altogether[9] and conclude with v.8. Yet, as Kümmel points out, "One could hardly have remained satisfied with a loss through the breaking off of a page; and none can see the reason for the conclusion being intentionally removed".[10] He believes "there is some probability that the *euangelion* of Mark 1:1 reached its climax at 16:7 and we therefore, have Mark entirely preserved".[11] However, in a thorough investigation of both the external and internal evidence, W. R. Farmer concludes that it leaves the matter 'still open', and that the best hope seems to lie in new papyrological discoveries, and in further progress in our understanding of the history of the development of text types emerging in the 2nd and 3rd centuries.[12]

Whatever the original conclusion of Mark may have been, we may confidently say that the Longer Ending does give evidence of a first-century belief in the Ascension[13] as an event consequent upon the Resurrection: "So then the Lord Jesus, after he had spoken to them, was received up into heaven, and sat down at the right hand of God" (Mark 16:19).

THE GOSPEL OF ST. JOHN

The writer of the Fourth Gospel has a dominant theme throughout, namely, that the Son has a special relation with the Father, emanates from him and returns to him, a journeying from the eternal to the temporal and back again by way of the Cross (13:3f).[14] The usage of "ascending", "journeying", "going", "departing[15]", plainly indicates that in the mind of the author, Jesus is on the way to the Father, and that believers are thereby brought into the presence of God to abide with him forever. The upward ascent is certainly in the mind of John in the two sentences, 3:13 "No one has ascended into heaven but he who descended from heaven, the Son of man[16]", and 6:62 "Then what if you were to see the Son of man ascending where he was before?"[17] (and possibly in 1:51 as well "...you will see heaven opened, and the angels of God ascending and descending upon the Son of man"). The two former as allusions to the Ascension are regarded by Swete as "the more significant because they are incidental[18]", but since they both refer to the Son of man, they are clearly important in relation to Christ and his followers. Of greatest importance are the words of the Risen Christ whom Mary encounters on Easter Day, saying, "Do not hold me, for I have not yet ascended to the Father; but go to my brethren and say to them, I am ascending to my Father and your Father, to my God and your God" (20:17). (*...oupo gar anabebēka pros ton Patera...Anabainō pros ton Patera*[19]).

In the first place, it is important to notice the use of the present tense *anabaino* "I am ascending" which suggests movement and continuity, even possibly a process leading to a climax.[20]

In the second place, it is quite plain that the Ascension has yet to take place, for "the Ascension still lies temporarily in the future. When the latter has happened, then it will be possible for Mary to touch the Lord, for new modes of touch will have become available. When was this accomplished?[21] Inasmuch as the Spirit cannot be given until Jesus is glorified (7:39), and inasmuch as the going up to the Father and the completion of the glorifying seem to be the same, it seems right to infer that before Jesus comes and breathes the Holy Spirit upon the Church on the evening of Easter Day, the Ascension has clearly happened".[22] The receiving of the Holy Spirit and the occasion when this actually happened, is dealt with in a subsequent chapter of this essay, but it suffices at this point to mention that, even if the Ascension did take place on the evening of Easter Day, there was a lapse of time between the Risen Lord's greeting to Mary, "early, while it was still dark" (20:1) and the impartation of the Holy Spirit through 'insufflation' – "He breathed on them, and said to them, 'Receive the Holy Spirit'" (20:22) "on the evening of that day" (20:19). Again, we see that once a time lapse *is* admitted, however brief in terms of hours or forty days, there is a definite distinction between the Resurrection and the Ascension, even if they appear to have taken place on Easter Day, as John would seem to portray. Furthermore, since John deliberately refers to the words of the Risen Christ which he spoke to Mary, indicating that the Ascension has yet to take place (in spite of the author's frequently bringing together events as a comprehensive whole), his very presentation of the scene in which he is risen but not yet ascended, makes them events which are separate and distinct, no matter how intimately they are related to each other. Professor C. K. Barrett, admitting the difficulty of *mē mou haptou oupō gar anabebēka pros ton Patera*

> "Do not touch me, I have not yet ascended to the Father" says "It was for John an essential act, completing what was done in the passion...in verse 22, the Spirit is given, and in verse 27, Thomas is invited to touch the Risen Christ. A possible conclusion is that in the ascension, complete glorification had taken place".[23] He continues, "But it must be admitted he does not say so, and it is very strange that so vital a fact should be left as a matter of inference. A more profitable line of interpretation is obtained when it is noted (Lagrange, 512) that the *de* which follows *poreuou* applies in effect to *anabainō*, the message to the brothers being parenthetical. The verse may then be paraphrased, 'Stop touching Me (or attempting to do so); it is true that I have not yet ascended to the Father but I am about to do so; – this is what you must tell my brothers'. This is perfectly intelligible. The resurrection has made possible a new and more spiritual union between Jesus and his disciples; the old physical contacts are no longer appropriate, though touch may yet (verse 27) be appealed to in proof that the glorified Lord is none other than he who was crucified".[24]

John's Gospel is primarily concerned with the fact of the Glory of God revealed in Jesus Christ, a theme which begins in the prologue and finds expression throughout the Fourth Gospel. Sometimes the redemptive events are all brought together, with one serving comprehensively for the others as in the words of Jesus when he made known that he was about to be betrayed, "When he (Judas) had gone out, Jesus said, 'Now is the Son of man glorified, and in him God is glorified; if God is glorified in him, God will also glorify him in himself, and glorify him at once'" (John 13:31f).[25] Earlier, it is recorded that Jesus had said, according to John "...the Spirit had not been given, because Jesus was not yet glorified" (7.39), clearly an anticipatory reference to the Cross wherein he is to be glorified and the Divine Seal of that glorification in the subsequent Resurrection and Exaltation. Therefore, we may believe that behind the theological interpretation of the later writing of John there lie the historical facts as the author knew them.[26] We may say with a degree of confidence that the Ascension "was for John an essential act, completing what was done in the passion",[27] and although it is not described as an observable incident as in Luke/Acts, it is nevertheless, the firm belief of John that after the Crucifixion, Jesus took his place at the Father's right hand in glory, having been raised from the dead by the glory of the Father (Rom. 6:4). C. K. Barrett sums it up when he says, with reference to the words "...it is to your advantage that I go away" (16:7) that "the Gospel itself consists in the fact that Jesus departs, for his departure means his death, his exaltation to heaven, and the coming of the Holy Spirit".[28]

THE PAULINE EPISTLES

The fact that Paul links his encounter with the Risen Christ on the Damascus Road with the post-resurrection appearances in 1 Cor. 15:8 has often led to the belief that he knew nothing of the Ascension whatsoever. Since the Pauline writings are the earliest evidence for the Resurrection, it has been assumed that the Ascension narrative is a later development of the Lucan writings to explain how the Risen Lord finally left this earth. Harnack is largely responsible for the introduction of this particular approach, and he has his modern counterpart in Bultmann who says,

> "The accounts of the empty grave, of which Paul still knows nothing, are legends. According to 1 Corinthians 15:5–8, where Paul enumerates the appearances of the risen Lord as tradition offered them, the resurrection of Jesus meant simultaneously his exaltation; not until later was the resurrection interpreted as a temporary return to life on earth, and the idea then gave rise to the ascension story (Luke 24:50–53; Acts 1:3–11)".[29]

It cannot be assumed that Paul's not mentioning the empty tomb necessarily implies his ignorance of it. As a Pharisee, he believed in the resurrection corporately, at the end of the age but he would not have thought of it as an individual experience at physical death. Yet, the use of *etaphē*[30] "was buried" (1 Cor. 15:4) shows that the Apostle would not have thought of the Resurrection of Jesus in any other way than of resurrection in body, and therefore of the tomb being left empty. It is, of course, in the nature of his approach that Resurrection and Exaltation are frequently brought together as seen in verses such as Romans

8:34; Colossians 3:1; Ephesians 1:20. Yet as Swete pointed out in connection with the verse in Romans,

> "Here are four well-marked links in a chain of facts – our Lord's death, resurrection, session, intercession. It is difficult to see why the second and the third, the Resurrection and the Session, should be taken as part of the same act, when the first is clearly distinct. If the Ascension is not mentioned, it is implied in the Session, for it is contrary to the usage of the New Testament to interpret *egeiresthai* of any exaltation beyond the mere recall from death".[31]

While it may be the normal practice to think of the two events as being held in the mind as one, and "natural to take Christ's resurrection and heavenly session as linked together"[32] as Ramsey remarks in relation to Col. 3:1 this is surely because the Apostle is using these events to illustrate the spiritual union of the believer with the Risen and Exalted Christ. He does this in similar fashion in Eph. 2:6 where he speaks of our being raised up with Christ and made to sit with him in the heavenly places, but in neither case can they be used to determine how Paul thought of these as original events or as a test of historical evidence. Referring to these two, Moule writes, "Of course, there are passages in the New Testament where resurrection and ascension are described as already belonging to Christians (Eph. 2:6, Col. 3:1, 3), but this is a matter of proleptic possession in Christ of what Christ has won".[33] The mentioning of the dual experience for Christians spiritually would strengthen, rather than weaken the argument for the two, resurrection and ascension, as being historically separate in the Apostle's thinking. The same applies to Eph. 1:20 as it relates to the believer's spiritual experience as a result of the resurrection and ascension of Christ.

Again, the concept of ascension is seen in Jesus' being "highly exalted" *huperupsoō* (Phil. 2:8f), as distinct from "being raised" *egertheis*(Rom. 6:9), and here, it is worthy of note that Paul moves directly from "death on a cross" to his being "highly exalted" without reference to the resurrection at all. Yet nobody reading the Pauline Epistles could fail to recognise how resurrection dominated all his thinking and experience as the opening words of his greatest letter show, "designated son of God in power according to the Spirit of holiness by his resurrection from the dead, Jesus Christ our Lord"[34] (Rom. 1:4). Although the *idea* of the descent of the Lord in his earliest letter would not necessarily imply an ascension, the fact that he uses *katabainō* stands in contrast to *anabainō*[35], and would suggest the former anticipating the latter.

The specific reference to ascension in Eph. 4:8–10 has led some to believe that the letter is post-Pauline[36] since it shows affinities with Luke-Acts. But the matter of the authorship of Ephesians is still a matter for debate, and in view of no finally convincing evidence having been produced to settle the question of authorship, the reference to the Ascension in the letter, in the light of what is noted earlier in this section, would not necessarily give grounds for rejecting the Pauline authorship of this letter.

The tradition of which Paul speaks in 1 Cor. 15:1f would almost certainly have been received from the Apostle Peter with whom he stayed for a fortnight (Gal. 1:18), and as a witness of the Ascension together with the other ten disciples, it is unlikely that Peter would have omitted to mention the Ascension in his conversation with Paul. Moreover, his speech at Pentecost does make a definite distinction between resurrection and ascension, (Acts 2:31, 34), and the Epistle of Peter, whether Petrine or by another hand writing under his name, refers to the Ascension in the words "through the resurrection of Jesus Christ, who has gone into heaven and is at the right hand of God..." (1 Peter 3:21f).

When we come to the Pastoral Epistles with the uncertainty as to whether they are entirely of Pauline authorship, part-Pauline, or other than Pauline in origin,[37] the reference to the Lord being "taken up in glory" *anelemphthē* (1 Tim. 3:16), would again seem to indicate that the author is aware of the Ascension.[38]

In this connection, it needs to be noted that the identical word is found in Acts 1:2, 22, and in 'Mark' 16:19 where, as we have seen, a clear distinction *is* drawn between resurrection and ascension.

As we shall see in the next main section of this essay, Paul's main contribution to our understanding of the Ascension lies rather in the *meaning* than the *mode*, as indeed, he is concerned with all the events in the life of Christ. This in no way implies his rejection of such events as being historical, but it *is* understandable that his chief interest should like in the theological, rather than the historical sphere, because his initial contact with Christ began with his encounter on the Damascus Road. As Moule says,

> "For him, the 'Lord from heaven' was the manner of his first experience of Jesus; and he naturally therefore, ranked the Damascus road experience, for that reason, side by side with the encounters which, for the Eleven and their companions, were the beginning of their knowledge of the Risen Lord. Never having known the Lord before the Crucifixion (not, at any rate, as a disciple knows him), St. Paul has no need to learn His heavenly, transcendental nature by a decisive withdrawal: the Lord was manifestly already 'in heaven'".[39]

If we take what are generally recognised as being the earliest and latest of Paul's letters, namely 1 Thessalonians and Philippians, we do have clear evidence of his belief in the Ascension. As Davies says,

> "The order of events could not have been more clearly expressed. First the Lord descends. Second, the dead rise, unquestionably to life on this earth since the third stage is that those who have risen, and those that are still alive are together 'caught up in the clouds, to meet the Lord in the air'. Resurrection is certainly not Ascension".[40] (1 Thess. 4:16f)

Then, with reference to his latest letter, Davies says, "When therefore, he tells the Philippians 'our citizenship is in heaven; from whence also we wait for a Saviour, the Lord Jesus Christ!' we may be confident that this and similar statements provide evidence of an Ascension"[41] (Phil. 3:20).

For the Apostle, the Ascension is as much a part of the 'exaltation-glorification' theme as is the Resurrection.[42] Indeed, it is true to say that for Paul, they are interdependent and certainly not mutually exclusive.

THE EPISTLE TO THE HEBREWS

The author of the Epistle to the Hebrews, in making the contrast between the insufficiency of the Old Testament sacrifies and the one full and sufficient sacrifice of Christ for sins for ever (7:27), regarding the former as the shadow of that which is to come in Christ (8:5), and his sacrifice as the real, sees Jesus as the One who, through his flesh (which is the veil), as the Forerunner and Pioneer, has prepared the way to the presence of the Father (10:19f). For the author, the concern is primarily theological, yet this in no way suggests that his interest in the historical is lacking.[43] Indeed, it is because of the historical fact of the Cross, emphasised throughout the Epistle, that he sees the way opened into the very presence of the Father (Cf:1:3, 8:1, 10:12, 12:2, *ekathisen* 'he sat down'), and (6:20, 9:12, 9:24, *eisēlthen* he entered), and "his theology causes him to dwell upon the death on Calvary and his entrance into heaven as the two stages in the imagery of sacrifice".[44] It is difficult to understand why, in 13:20, which is the only reference to the resurrection in the whole Epistle (*ho anagagōn ek nekrōn*)[45] this would specifically be mentioned if he did not wish to remind readers of the historical fact of the resurrection and the exaltation as being separate and distinctive. Even if the reference in 13:20 were not included, it would still be necessary to assume that the author did not think of the Crucified as having passed directly from the Cross into heaven without his first having been raised from the dead to life again. Justin says that Jesus "was crucified and ascended into heaven" (*staurōthenai kai anabebēkenai eis ton ouranon*),[46] but nodbody imagines that he was unaware of the Resurrection and that the Ascension was consequent upon, and subsequent to, the former as a separate event. The bringing together of major events such as these in the life of our Lord is seen to be an accommodation of language and ideas, and not the means whereby the historical origins can be ascertained and tested.

THE FIRST EPISTLE OF ST. PETER

The dominant theme of the First Epistle of St. Peter is that of the Resurrection of Jesus Christ by which believers have been born anew, and on earth anticipate, especially in time of suffering and persecution, their redemption and entrance into heaven (1 Peter 1:3f). For the writer (whatever view we take of his identity), Jesus Himself, having been raised from the dead is now at the right hand of the Father, and the fact of Peter's referring to the "angels, authorities and powers subject to him" (3:22b), is an indication that he is now the Exalted Lord.[47] Yet, the mentioning of the Resurrection and his going into heaven in 3:21, 22a (*poreutheis eis ouranon*), surely suggests two separate events which the author wishes to be brought to the attention of the reader.[48] Jesus goes to the Father by way of the Cross, the Resurrection and the Ascension into heaven, to be exalted at the right hand of God.

REVELATION OF ST. JOHN THE DIVINE

The whole of the Apocalypse centres around the Glorified and Exalted Lord who will eventually come to create a new heaven and a new earth (21:1f). Meanwhile, he who sits upon the throne says "Behold, I make all things new" (21:5); he is worshipped by all the host of heaven unceasingly (7:9f); he is "King of kings and Lord of lords" (19:16), and even now shares his Father's throne (3:21). "Through His Ascension, He has become ruler of the kings of the earth" (1:5).[49] It is to him that the two witnesses ascend in a cloud (*anebēsan eis ton ouranon en tē nephelē*), which are unmistakeable references to the Ascension by the phrase, "they went up to heaven in a cloud" (11:12). Both the words *anebēsan* and *nephelē*, suggest association with Luke's account of the Ascension.

For while the Ascension is most certainly, first and foremost a Christological happening, it does have distinct relation to believers as the Seer tells in their sharing in the victory of Christ when he writes, "He who conquers I will grant him to sit with me on my throne, as I myself conquered and sat down with my Father on his throne" (3:21). Further, he is the "male child...caught up to God and to his throne" (12:5),[50] and while we are, of course, dealing here in symbolic ideas and language, it nevertheless, does employ the concept of ascension which must have emanated primarily from Christ's Ascension, and possibly from Paul's earlier writing in which he states that "then we who are alive, who are left, shall be caught up together with them in the clouds to meet the Lord in the air; and so we shall always be with the Lord" (1 Thess. 4:17). The Ascension certainly seems to have influenced the thinking of the author of the Apocalypse when he portrays the vision given to him of the Christ who is alive for evermore (1:18).

CONCLUSION

Our survey and critical analysis of relevant passages of the New Testament can leave no doubt that references to the Ascension are by no means confined to the Lucan narratives in both the Gospel and the Acts of the Apostles, but are found to be present, by implication, in the four Gospels: (anticipation in St. Matthew, confirmation with the 'Marcan' Longer Ending in the first century, and theological interpretation in St. John); in the Pauline Epistles (including the Ephesians, whoever the author may have been), the epistle to the Hebrews, the Pastorals whether of Pauline or other authorship); in 1 Peter and in the Apocalypse. To look for a uniformity of interpretation would prove to be a vain quest, but since Christians believe that the Crucified Lord was raised again, as the New Testament so clearly states, and without which there would not have been a Gospel at all, then the Lord who was raised from the tomb and who appeared with the evidence of crucifixion in his body (however transformed and glorified), must have left this earth at some point for the unseen and eternal world. The New Testament saw Psalm 16:8f as prophetic of Christ's Resurrection as cited by Peter on the Day of Pentecost (Acts 2:25f), and then follows with reference to Psalm 110:1 referring to the Ascension (Acts 2:34f). The alternative has been well stated by Milligan when he says "If the Lord Jesus did die again, where and under what circumstances did His death take place?...was He alone or surrounded by His friends? What was the last message sent by Him to his disciples?...to none of these questions can a reply be given".[51] Answering these questions he poses, and related questions, Milligan continues thus:

> "If there be sufficient proof that Jesus rose from the grave, the unbeliever has no interest in denying the Ascension; and, on the other hand, the believer has no need to ask more in order to satisfy himself that the Ascension really happened. From the very nature of the case, he must conclude that, if our Lord rose from the dead and that in a glorified condition, He could neither have continued to live as an inhabitant of this earth nor have again died. In one way or another, He must have passed into the spiritual and eternal world, and must have returned to His God and Father. Any difficulties connected with this evidence may be ascribed to our imperfect knowledge of the circumstances; the reality of the fact itself may be accepted without hesitation".[52]

If we pause to reflect upon the fact of what did happen to the Body of Jesus, "only one of two things could have happened. Either the body of Christ was physically raised or it physically rotted".[53] and we simply cannot dismiss these alternatives as being insignificant or merely a matter of local concern.[54] Readily, of course, we accept that the Resurrection was not the resuscitation of a corpse, but was rather "death won by New Man",[55] and further, that it is 'metahistorical'[56] as Professor Turner defines it, since it is both within history and beyond history, (for, as he says, "the gospel message includes both history and faith"[57]), yet to omit, or attempt to exclude the former, would be false to the testimony of the New Testament. And if the Scriptures reveal that the resurrection body of Jesus "was at once sufficiently corporeal to show his wounds, and sufficiently immaterial to pass through closed doors",[58] then there must have come a time when such revelation concluded and He finally departed from visible sight. Luke alone tells us *in narrative* form how the Risen Christ left this earth, and even he is far from being crudely literalistic since the post-Resurrection appearances he records, like those elsewhere in the New Testament, are fully shown to be of a Risen Lord in His "spiritual body" (*sōma pneumatikon*) which is elaborated and elucidated in Paul's extended treatment by illustrating from nature itself (cf:1 Cor. 15:35f). It is in this spiritual body that Jesus ascends to his Father, and his going, journeying, departing, entering, being received up, and his ascending, all imply his leaving this world and being no longer seen by witnesses. Readily, we acknowledge that "the Ascension as an event in time is definitely part of the Christian tradition".[59]

In 1892, Milligan wrote words which find their parallel in 1973 when, under the heading 'True Record', in The Church Times, the leading article said,

> "The timing of Easter is determined by reference to the Passover moon; the Ascension by the exact interval which elapsed between Easter and its occurrence. To ignore this factor might well encourage the contemporary tendency to argue that both Resurrection and Ascension are not historical at all, but must be viewed as 'myths' of one kind or another. A great deal of intellectual energy has gone into this argument in recent years. The historical evidence may indeed be hard to come by, and certainty about details may remain elusive. But what is certain is that either the tomb was empty, or it was not; either the Risen Lord spoke with his disciples, or he did not; *either he ascended in their sight or he did not* (italics mine). These things are either truth or lies. There is really no half-way house possible".[60]

Here we are at the very heart of our faith, in spite of all the mystery which surrounds it, for without the Ascension, a hiatus exists whereby the Jesus of history and the Christ of faith are virtually unrelated to each other. The Ascension is the essential link between the Jesus who walked this earth and the Lord of heaven, the Christ who entered our world of time and space and now reigns in glory in the eternal world, the Saviour who died on Calvary's Cross and the High Priest who ever lives to make intercession in heaven for his people on earth. The Ascension is seen to be that focal point of the New Testament which the subsequent chapters of this essay now seek to interpret.

PART TWO

Theological Evaluation of the Ascension

CHAPTER THREE

The Exaltation of Jesus Christ

Our examination of the relevant passages in the New Testament has revealed that a distinction is made between the Resurrection and the Ascension, even though the narrative of the latter is to be found only in the Lucan writings. The distinction lies in the fact that, when Jesus was raised from the grave, he had conquered death, but when he ascended into heaven, his entrance was the sign of his being exalted to the Father's Right Hand on high. And even if Resurrection and Ascension are frequently held together as one event by the majority of New Testament authors, the fact that his Resurrection took place on earth would not have conveyed the impression that he was also the Exalted One unless he had also been taken up to heaven into the glory of the presence of his Father.

> "It is, however, of profound significance that the New Testament distinguishes the resurrection from the exaltation of Christ. As the Risen One, Christ would only be the first-fruit from the dead, the firstborn among many brethren. There would be no fundamental difference between His resurrection and ours. His Lordship would be inconceivable apart from His resurrection, but it would not be accounted for by it alone. For this reason, the New Testament draws a logical distinction between the resurrection and the exaltation[1]".

And since for the writers of the New Testament, any concept of a spiritual triumph would necessarily include the body sharing in such victory, it implies that being raised in body meant being exalted in body too. As Benoit says,

> "It is then certain enough that for Paul, it is in his body that Christ is glorified and lives in heaven; and no less certain that he had to ascend there corporeally after issuing from the tomb. If the Apostle does not feel the need to enunciate this explicitly, it remains nevertheless presupposed. And if he does happen to allude to it, as in Ephesians 4:10, it is in a context of cosmological thought which plainly includes the physical reality of his glorious ascent to the highest of the heavenly spheres[2]".

Furthermore, the emphasis of the Ascension (or Assumption) of Christ is one of the Divine action of the Father; it is an *analēmpsis* and emphasises, like the Resurrection, that it is the Father who always takes the initiative.[3] While agreeing with Benoit on the one point just mentioned, we cannot accept his view that the Ascension was simply Christ's condescension to the disciples to demonstrate that the Christophanies had now come to an end when he says, "We are not watching a glorious triumph; not colours of a theophany, no voice from heaven, no shining vestments as at Baptism and Transfiguration. If lacking, is this not simply because Luke is not describing a triumph but only the last scene of farewell[4]?" The fact that Christ is being taken up, the fulfilment of the exaltation anticipated in Luke 9:51, the mention of the cloud which would symbolise the Divine Glory, the two men in white robes could not but lead the witnesses of the Ascension to think that it was none other than the occasion of Christ entering into his glory in the presence of the Father.[5]

All concepts of the Exaltation inevitably go back to Psalm 110:1, "The Lord says to my lord: Sit at my right hand, till I make your enemies your footstool".[6] It is cited more than any other Old Testament passage[7] – a fact remarkable in itself thus showing where the emphasis of the New Testament really lies – and is "so common as to be reported without direct reference"[8] as is seen in the "powers subject to him" (1 Peter 3:22), which clearly has this Psalm in mind.[9] Moreover, the New Testament Church readily saw in the Old Testament Coronation Psalms an appropriate application to the Exaltation of Christ, notably Psalms 24, 47, 68, 110, 118, and referring to these Psalms, Argyle says that "whatever the original application of these passages may have been, the early Christians saw in them a prediction fulfilled in the triumph and exaltation of Jesus".[10] Taking the first four of these Psalms in their application to the

Ascension of Christ, Davies gives their Old Testament background as being appropriate to the exaltation of Christ when he writes, "It is to be noted that each of these Psalms which were applied by Christian writers to the Ascension had been referred by one scholar or another to this festival (that is the autumnal Festival of the Jewish New Year which celebrated the enthronement of Yahweh as universal King), and indeed, Dr. W. O. E. Oesterley and Dr. A. R. Johnson have linked all four with this celebration".[11] Davies then sets out the four stages in this Israelite New Year, showing how they were applied to the Ascension of Christ, and which can be conveniently summarised in the following manner:-

(a) The procession ascended the hill of Zion and escorted both the ark of Yahweh and the Davidic King into the Temple precincts;

(b) A ritual combat which re-enacted the triumph of Yahweh and of his anointed representatives over the forces of death and chaos;

(c) A re-enthronement of Yahweh as King over the contemporary ruler;

(d) The sacred marriage.

Their application to the Ascension of Christ is as follows:-

(a) Christ ascended on high and entered heaven itself (Heb. 9:24).

(b) Triumph over evil – "He who conquers...as I myself conquered...sat down with my Father on his throne" (Rev. 3:21)

(c) Enthronement as the Lord's Anointed – "We have such a high priest, one who is seated at the right hand of the throne of the Majesty in heaven" (Heb. 8:1) being "designated by God a high priest after the order of Melchizedek" (Heb. 5:10).

(d) "Lord of lords and King of kings" (Rev. 17:19).[12]

Davies further points out that, since three of these Psalms in the LXX translation use the verb *anabainō* which is applied to Christ's Ascension, they are justifiably used by Christian writers with reference to his Ascension, as its meaning is always a movement from a lower to a higher plane.[13]

The Ascension is primarily a Christological event,[14] declaring that, whereas the Resurrection means Jesus lives, the Ascension asserts that he reigns.[15] He is the Christ "whom heaven must receive until the time for establishing all that God spoke by the mouth of his holy prophets from old" (Acts 3:21); whom "God exalted...at his right hand as Leader and Saviour" (Acts 5:3) whom "God has made...both Lord and Christ" (Acts 2:36); and who, "became obedient unto death, even death on a cross, therefore God has highly exalted him" (Phil. 2:8f) *huperupsōsen*. Although Jesus had equality with the Father, something he did not grasp at,[16] it was on account of his obedience to the point of death that the "ascension is regarded as the chronological beginning point of his lordship",[17] for as Cullmann reminds us, after his death, Jesus did not simply return to the form of existence he already had for he has now entered a still closer relationship with God who confers upon him the title Kurios with full lordship over all.[18] And since Kurios is the Old Testament equivalent of Adonai, the alternative name of God being Yahweh, the Exalted Christ receives the equality of God himself, given him by the Father. Already the Son of God in power *endunamei* (Rom. 1:4) by virtue of his Resurrection, he is now made Lord and Christ (Acts 2:36) by virtue of his Ascension.[19]

Since the Ascension is seen to be the Exaltation of Jesus as Lord, it might be thought that it is possible to think of the Being of God dualistically, yet this is clearly avoided by the Apostle stating that his Exaltation to Lordship is "to the glory of God the Father" (Phil. 2:11). It is God who has exalted him (*dio kai* 'that is why'), and the "*hina* safeguards monotheism"[20] since his lordship covers the age between the Ascension and the time "when he delivers the kingdom to God the Father after destroying every rule and every authority and power" (1 Cor. 15:24). As Cullmann points out, all titles except that of Father which are applied to God are also applied to Christ, even that of Creator,[21] but it is in his Exaltation that the Lordship of Jesus is a present fact, consequent upon the Ascension. Christians rightly believe in the future reign of Christ because of his present reign, and but await the day of his open victory.[22]

The Ascended Christ is spoken of as having been exalted to the right hand of the Father, and this implies dignity and honour, rather than location, though the latter cannot be ruled out entirely as being without meaning since our human limitations compel us to think in categories of space and time. Nevertheless, we fully recognise that the phrase 'the right hand of God' is metaphorical language for divine omnipotence and omnipresence, and that it affirms he is reigning everywhere as King and Lord, wielding the power of divine authority.[23] Moreover, as Barth observes, the past tense is used of all other actions of Christ whereas the present tense is applied when speaking of 'He sits'.[24] Such symbolical and picture language, when recognised as such, avoids the two extremes of being naively literalistic on the one hand, and falling into the vagueness of generalities on the other hand whereby the Figure of the Glorified and Exalted Lord would cease to be portrayed as personal.[25]

THE SON OF MAN

The New Testament makes plain that "Jesus is unique, not so much in the outward pattern of His life...as in the fact that after His earthly ministry, He was exalted to heaven, there to rule at God's right hand",[26] and that he did anticipate such exaltation[27] is heard in his reply to Caiaphas at his Trial (Mark 14:62 cf: Matthew 26:64 and Luke 22:69). These words, being a combination of Daniel 7:13 where "one like a son of man...came to the Ancient of Days", and Psalm 110:1, telling of the Exalted Lord at the right hand of God, form the reply given at a time of great emotional stress,[28] and expressing both exaltation and identity. These two vitally important characteristics are included in the phrase, the Son of Man which occurs frequently in the Gospels as a favourite self-description of our Lord. The immediacy expressed in the variant forms of introducing the sentences in both Matthew and Luke (*ap'arti* and *apo tou nūn* respectively)[29] which may also have stood in the Marcan version,[30] does show that "the meaning of Jesus' reply would therefore seem to be that, although He was about to be put to a shameful death, He was really entering upon His reign (cf: Phil. 2:8–11)...the teaching and ministry of Jesus confirm the view that He faced the Cross with the conviction that it was not defeat, but the gateway to His glory".[31]

The term 'the Son of Man', which has implications more radical than political Messiahship,[32] is applied to the Exalted Lord as the unique Son of God, and

> "it may be said that it is only after His exaltation when He comes in glory, that Jesus becomes the Son of Man. With some justification, it has been said that, during His earthly life, He was a prospective Messiah; and therefore, it might be said, with greater justification, that he was a prospective Son of Man. But, according to the

testimony of the Gospels, Jesus also applied the term, 'the Son of Man' to Himself as He was...in every way, a man among men".[33]

Here we have the great paradox of the Person of Jesus – the Unique Son of God, fully aware of his special relation with God as the only begotten Son of the Father; of his being the Son of Man who "must be lifted up" (John 3:14), with its obvious reference to both his death and his exaltation; and, at the same time, his choice of a phrase which is both representative and inclusive, so that whatever happens to him must ultimately concern all those who believe in him; "whoever believes in him may have eternal life" (John 3:15). He is therefore, seen to be the Corporate Christ who, have identified himself with mankind, sharing our flesh and blood (Heb. 2:14) is the Son of Man, a title which Jesus appears to have taken from Daniel and not from the Similitudes of Enoch – and there seems to be no reason for suggesting that he never actually applied it to himself – to whom is "given dominion and glory and a kingdom, that all peoples, nations, and languages should serve him" (Daniel 7:14). The very setting and usage clearly indicate that Jesus thought of himself as being both unique in his relation to the Father and as Representative of the human race. "As Daniel 7 now stands", writes Moule, "(whatever the stages of its composition), *the saints are symbolised by the Human One* – not identified with, but represented by him: and if the saints are partially and temporarily eclipsed, only to be subsequently glorified, then exactly the same may be presumed to be appropriately predicted of the Human Figure. If so, then the 'Son of Man' already means 'the representative of God's chosen people, destined through suffering to be exalted'".[34] And, since the Son of Man comes *to* the Ancient of Days, it means exaltation for him, and through him, for his people too![35] Similarly, C. H. Dodd stresses both the uniqueness and the identity of Christ with his people in the use of the term when he says,

"The Johannine Son of Man is the Son of God; He descended from heaven and ascends to heaven again (iii.13; vi.62, etc.). He is in intimate union with God, 'dwelling in Him'. He is archetypal at least in the sense that His relation to the Father is the archtype of the true and ultimate relation of men to God...the Hellenistic heavenly Man, dwelling either in all men, or in those who are *teleioi anthrōpoi* represents, or sums up in Himself, humanity as such...as Son of

Man he is in some sort the inclusive representative of Ideal or redeemed humanity. He descends into the world and dies in order that He may draw all men to Him (xii.32). He ascends to God in order that where He is, they may be also (xiv.13). For this conception of the solidarity of believers with Christ, there was precedent in the Christian tradition. Not only is it impressively worked out in Paul's doctrine of the Body of Christ but it is implied in such Synoptic sayings as Matthew xxv.40...'Inasmuch as you did it to one of the least of these my brethren, you did it to me'; Matt. x.49, 'He who receives you, receives me'; Luke x.16 'He who hears you hears me, and he who rejects you rejects me'. This is one of the few Synoptic sayings which have a close parallel in the Fourth Gospel; xiii.20, 'He who receives whomsoever I send receives me'. Such solidarity is a part of what the Fourth Evangelist means by describing Christ as Son of Man".[36]

The sense of the Christian being incorporated into the Crucified, Risen and Exalted Christ and Saviour is implied, both as a spiritual experience now, and as an anticipated hope which finds fulfilment hereafter in the Apostle's words when he writes, "But God, who is rich in mercy, out of the great love with which he loved us, even when we were dead through our trespasses, made us alive together with Christ (by grace you have been saved), and raised us up with him, and made us sit with him in the heavenly places in Christ Jesus, that in the coming ages he might show the immeasurable riches of his grace in kindness toward us in Christ Jesus" (Eph. 2:4f).[37]

We find therefore, that the term Son of Man, provides the link between Christ and ourselves, since it implies not only his exaltation through suffering but also his identity with mankind, and therefore, the exaltation of believers in and through his redemptive work, once and for all on earth, the effects of which are forever continued through the Intercessory Ministry of the Ascended Christ.

CHAPTER FOUR

The Heavenly Intercession

The Ascended Lord is the King who is exalted at the Father's right hand, sharing the throne of heaven with his Father (Revelation 3:21), and, at the same time, is the "eldest among a large family of brothers" (Romans 8:29 N.E.B.). His Ascension means that he has taken our humanity, which he assumed at the Incarnation, to the very throne of the Godhead, and there he wears it, nevermore to lay it aside[1]. Indeed, he shares the throne of the Father himself and promises to share it with his followers who have conquered (Revelation 3:21), for his Exaltation means, not his escape from humanity[2], but his eternal union with mankind as Representative Man, who "always lives to make intercession for them" (Heb. 7:25). He can do so, because he "has entered...into heaven itself, now to appear in the presence of God on our behalf" (Heb. 9:24).

While the theme of the High Priesthood of Christ is found more in the Epistle to the Hebrews[3] than elsewhere, it is by no means confined to it. "That Christ continues his work since his exaltation is by no means a 'Catholic' invention, but a fundamental idea of the whole New Testament. It was just for this reason...that the Gospel of John was written...above all in this context, we must speak of a Christological concept which points primarily to the exalted Christ. It is the concept Jesus as Lord. Its importance for early Christianity cannot be overstated".[4]

The Christ exalted at the Father's right hand; "he sat down at the right hand of the Majesty on high" (Heb. 1:3); we have such a high priest, one who is seated at the right hand of the throne of the Majesty in heaven" (Heb. 8:1); "when Christ had offered for all time a single sacrifice for sins, he sat down at the right hand of God" (Heb. 10:12); "Jesus...endured the cross...and is seated at the right hand of the throne of God" (Heb. 12:2); – is the Heavenly Intercessor who is "seated on the throne of that heavenly world which is above us and around us on every side, (and) is One in whom the human nature has been closely and indissolubly united with the Divine...at the Ascension, the goal of humanity is reached".[5]

In the Passion and Death of Christ, we see him as both Victim and Victor, the Priest who offers the Sacrifice of himself, and his High Priesthood is therefore, seen as beginning at the Ascension with the "consummation of His priestly service...found in His perpetual intercession in heaven".[6] He it is, of whom it is written, "Thou art a priest for ever, after the order of Melchizedek" (Heb. 7:17), with the explanation earlier in the chapter that Melchizedek "is without father or mother or genealogy, and has neither beginning of days nor end of life, but resembling the Son of God he continues a priest for ever" (Heb. 7:3); the One who "holds his priesthood permanently, because he continues for ever" (Heb. 7:24), and who "consequently...is able for all time to save those who draw near to God through him, since he always lives to make intercession for them" (Heb. 7:25). Argyle sums it up when he says, "Since He is King and Priest forever, His intercession is permanent, and He can carry through His pleading triumphantly to its absolute completion (*eis to pantelēs*)".[7]

The Sacrifice offered on Calvary was "once for all when he offered up himself" (Heb. 7:27), and it is therefore, unrepeatable, unique, absolute and final. Yet, if we go on to ask what is the relation between the heavenly priesthood and Calvary, the reply is that the act of sacrifice is over, but *The Sacrifice*, Christ himself, forever remains, in the way that with the Old Testament sacrifices, the blood stood upon the altar after the victim had been slain.[8] Jesus therefore, as High Priest in heaven offers himself on our behalf, not in any sense of repeating the Sacrifice made on earth,

> "but His presence in the Holiest is a perpetual and effective presentation before God of the Sacrifice once offered, *which is no less needful for our acceptance than the actual death upon the Cross* (italics

mine)...He offers Himself as representing to God man reconciled, and as claiming for men the right of access to the Divine presence. He Himself, as He sits on the Throne, in the perfected and glorified Manhood which has been obedient unto death, is the living Propitiation for our sins, and the standing guarantee of acceptance to all that draw near unto God through Him (Heb. 7:25)".[9]

The Intercessory life in heaven of the Ascended, Exalted Lord is something more than prayer, for it is the total life of himself, offered on behalf of, and entering into his people at every point, and in every circumstance on earth. "We are" says Milligan,

> "to understand it of every act by which the Son, in dependence on the Father, in the Father's Name, whatever He Himself enjoys in the communications of His Father's love may become also theirs...He goes to Him, not as one between whom and God a gulf had to be bridged, or as if He were asking aid from an external source He goes to Him in the full consciousness of mutual love; in that Divine fellowship in which He knows that the will of the Father is His Will; and, in which, therefore He has only to utter thoughts that belong in common to the ineffable unity of Their common life. But, so going, he prays".[10]

This is an emphasis which has been sadly lacking for some time, and which, has contemporary relevance in every age. The Christ whom we worship is not only a Living and Reigning Lord, but One who continually enters into the life of his people in every situation, because as the Ascended Christ, he is no longer confined or restricted by earthly limitations, but touches life at every point and concerns himself with the whole of human affairs and existence. His is "the name which is above every name" (Phil. 2:9), and it is worthy of note that after the Ascension narrative in Acts 1, the subsequent chapters show how the Ascended and Exalted Lord is set forth in terms of his Name, and it is in his Name that salvation is to be found (Acts 2:21; 4:12 etc.); miracles are performed in his Name (3:16; 4:10); and preaching was in the Name of Jesus (5:40f), so that even when persecuted, "they left the presence of the council, rejoicing that they were counted worthy to suffer dishonour for the name" (5:41). Luke virtually replaces the traditional idea of intercession of the Exalted Lord by 'the Name', and "we can go so far as to say that to speak of the efficacy of the name is Luke's way of describing the presence of Christ"[11] among his people on earth.

Believing therefore, that the Ascended Lord is always interceding on behalf of his people in terms, not only of praying but of entering into their life on earth, it can never be imagined that to talk of the Heavenly Intercession is something remote, abstract, aloof and unrelated to everyday life and circumstances, or as being something simply of interest to the theologian or even those who are called to live the monastic life. Swete aptly expressed it when he said, "It is so real and falls so well within the range of Christian experience that every believer can test for himself the truth of our Lord's work in heaven, however little he can discern its nature. Communion with God through Christ in the Holy Spirit is not a theory or a dogma, but a fact of personal knowledge to which tens of thousands of living Christians can testify as the most certain of actualities".[12]

The recognition of the full meaning of the Heavenly Intercession brings the Cross of Christ into true perspective for it is seen as being, both an event in time and as something of eternal significance. The following lines of Michael Bruce show the historical and the contemporary as being held together through the Heavenly Intercession:-

He who for men their surety stood,
And poured on earth His precious blood,
Pursues in heaven His mighty plan,
The Saviour and the friend of man.

Though now ascended up on high,
He bends on earth a brother's eye;
Partaker of the human name,
He knows the frailty of our frame.[13]

We could not do better than conclude this section of our study by quoting again from Swete, for he brings an emphasis to our attention which for far too long has been neglected. Indeed, it might well be asked if it ever has had the emphasis it should, for too often, the Heavenly Intercession has been either largely ignored, or else too narrowly defined. This, it would seem, is accounted for by the neglect of the Ascension of which it is a constituent part, and a renewed interest in the latter would most surely result in a reappraisal of the vital importance of the Heavenly Intercession in our day. Swete says,

> "No aspect of our Lord's heavenly life is more to be insisted upon than His priestly office and work. Popular theology on all sides, shews a tendency to stop short at the Cross, that is, at the historical moment when the Divine Sacrifice was offered. The blessings of our redemption are traced to the Passion...as to suggest that they would have been ours if Christ had neither risen from the dead nor ascended into heaven...with St. Paul, not the Cross and Passion, but the Ascension and the High Priestly Intercession are the climax of our Lord's saving work (Romans 8:34)".[14]

Each age tends to stress either the transcendence or the immanence of the Person of Christ, either his divinity or his humanity, his presence in heaven, or, through the Holy Spirit, his presence on earth. Biblical theology shows that it is not a matter of either/or, but of both/and, and the doctrine of the Ascension of Christ, standing at the junction of history and eternity, sight and faith, earth and heaven, maintains a right balance in our understanding of the Person of Christ for all time. Such understanding, with its emphasis upon otherworldliness and the affairs of this earth, with the Christ who reigns in Glory and who, at the same time, is remote from none,[15] save in so far as men refuse to acknowledge his Kingdom and Rule in their lives and that of society, could well lead to a renewed experience of spiritual regeneration in our day. The Apostle's prayer has particular relevance in this connection when he writes, "that acording to the riches of his glory he may grant you to be strengthened with might through his Spirit in the inner man, and that Christ may dwell in your hearts through faith; that you, being rooted and grounded in love, may have power to comprehend with all the saints what is the breadth and length and height and depth, and to know the love of Christ which surpasses knowledge, that you may be filled with all the fulness of God" (Eph. 3:16f).

CHAPTER FIVE

The Holy Spirit

The New Testament makes it plain that the descent of the Holy Spirit is consequent upon the exaltation of Jesus, for it is when Jesus is glorified that the Spirit is given (John 7:39). And, as Lindsay Dewar says, since "the doctrine of the Holy Spirit is essentially a *Christian* doctrine...it led to the expectation that there would be an outpouring of the Holy Spirit in the last days, thus making the New Testament doctrine of the Holy Spirit 'eschatological[1]'". This eschatological emphasis is seen in the event of Pentecost when Peter explains that the strange phenomenon witnessed on that occasion is none other than the fulfilment of the last days as prophesied by Joel in the gift of the Holy Spirit being outpoured by the Ascended Lord and Christ (Acts 2:15–36). It is only when Christ is "lifted up" (John 12:32)[2] from the earth only after the time when he goes to the Father (cf. John 16:7), that the Holy Spirit is given.

A difficulty arises when we ask at what precise point the Holy Spirit was given to the disciples since there are two accounts of the Spirit being given; the first by the Risen Christ on Easter Evening when he said, "Receive the Holy Spirit" (John 20:22) and the second being the Day of Pentecost when it is clearly stated, "Being therefore exalted at the right hand of God, and having received from the Father the promise of the Holy Spirit, he has poured out this which you see and hear". (Acts 2:33).

If the Resurrection and the Exaltation are taken together as one event on a single occasion, the difficulty is immediately eliminated as to the timing of the occasion of the giving of the

Holy Spirit, since the Risen Christ, appearing on the evening of Easter Day breathes on his disciples, and they receive the Spirit from the One who is both risen and ascended.[3] Yet, while the one difficulty is removed, another is created since it raises the question as to the historicity of Luke's account of the giving of the Spirit at Pentecost in Acts 2.[4] Ramsey thinks that "a twofold action may have occurred in the redemptive events on Easter Day, a bestowal of the breath of new life; at Pentecost, an outpouring for the execution of those tasks which the new life involved",[5] whereas Swete believes that the gift was given proleptically, so that the word of Jesus on Easter Evening becomes a promise of the descent of the Holy Spirit later on, in the way in which the promise was given by the Ascending Christ in both the Lucan narratives (Luke 24:49, Acts 1:4f). This seems to be a real possibility, except that to render the aorist imperative *Labete Pneuma Hagion* "you will receive" as Theodore of Mopsuestia[6] suggested, instead of the future indicative, does create difficulties where the tense of the verb is concerned. Swete, fully aware of this fact himself observes, "As for the imperative, it is a warning against a merely passive attitude on the part of those who receive the gifts of Christ...this gift, though given absolutely to the Church, belongs to individual believers only so far by an act of the will they severally lay hold upon it and appropriate to their own use".[7] But perhaps the most satisfactory explanation is that of R. Newton Flew who says,

> "Both agree in the supreme fact that the Spirit is given by Jesus Himself after the Resurrection. According to John, who has no account of the Ascension (though he presupposes it, 6:62; 20:17), this takes place on the first Easter Day; according to Luke, on the fiftieth day. In view of the fact that the other accounts of the Resurrection appearances tell us nothing of the gift of the Spirit on the day of the Resurrection, the Lucan narrative is to be preferred".[8]

This seems acceptable, particularly when it is remembered that the Johannine chronology, as distinct from his history, differs considerably from the Synoptic Gospels on a number of occasions. With his primary interest in the theological interpretation, and his frequently bringing together historical happenings portraying an exalted and glorified Christ and Lord, it is not surprising that for him, it is the Risen Christ who imparts the Holy Spirit to his disciples.[9]

THE INTERCESSION OF CHRIST AND OF THE HOLY SPIRIT

Of particular interest is that the Ascended Christ who intercedes in heaven and the Holy Spirit who intercedes within the life of the believer (Romans 8:26f), have the closest possible relation to each other, while at the same time, they are seen to be theologically distinguishable. As Milligan says, "It is in the idea of representation that the two designations meet. Jesus glorified represents us before the Father's throne; the Holy Spirit abiding with us represents in us Jesus gone to the Father."[10]

The experience of the Holy Spirit brings us into contact in this way, with the Ascended Lord and Christ, and avoids any interpretation of the Spirit which is separate from, and unrelated to, the Person of Christ. Indeed, it does bring all 'spiritual' experience to be tested by the historical revelation of God in Christ, and, as Cave so fittingly writes, "The Spirit gave to men, not new revelations, but the rediscovery of the revelation given in Jesus Christ. The highest knowledge that the Spirit gives is knowledge of the mind of Christ (1 Cor. 2:16)".[11]

Since the Holy Spirit, the gift of the Ascended Christ, indwells the believer, we may therefore rightly assume that his chief work is to form Christ in us (Gals. 4:19), so that we may become like him and see him as he is (1 John 3:3). In this way, "Christ's own Spirit, the Spirit by which His humanity has been moulded into what it is, passes into His people, so passing into them as to pervade every part of what they are. What can the effect be but the revelation and formation of Christ Himself within them?"[12] For it is through the gift of the Spirit that we are enabled, not only to see the Divine Glory in Christ, but also the Father's ultimate purpose for mankind. It is by the transforming work of the Holy Spirit that we become what God intends us to be, and "the more we are brought to share in Christ's glory, the more shall we share in that giving glory to the Father which was His mission and is our calling."[13] The intercessory ministry of Christ is a continuing activity through the Holy Spirit's indwelling his people until at length they become complete and entire in him at his appearing.[14]

THE ASCENDED CHRIST AND HIS CHURCH

The Acts of the Apostles begins with the account of Christ's ascending to the Father, moving on immediately to show how through him, the Ascended Lord and Christ, the Holy Spirit is sent forth, and this in turn inaugurates the story of the Christian Church. Furthermore, since the Holy Spirit is seen as a personal gift to his people, we find at the same time that the words, *saint*, *king* and *priest*, are always applied to believers in the plural,[15] whereas they are applied to Christ alone in the singular. This is a clear indication that the Spirit is a corporate gift from Christ, and therefore, one cannot think of the Ascension and the consequent gift of the Spirit without at the same time, thinking of the Church, the Body of Christ of which the Ascended Lord is the Head. Equally, it is not possible to think of the Church without reference to the Exalted Head and Lord.[16] As Torrance says, "We cannot pay too much attention to the fact that the Holy Spirit was sent upon the Church after the Crucifixion, Resurrection and Ascension of Christ. In that series, Pentecost belongs as one of the mighty salvation events, and to that series, the parousia will belong to the last".[17]

As he points out, the Body of Christ is the all important metaphor whereby the Church is described as having the closest possible relation to the Beloved Son, yet it is through the Ascension that Christ has "distanced"[18] himself from his Church, for "the Cross stands between".[19] Again, "in being the Body of Christ, the Church meets her Lord; she does not prolong Him, but she expresses Him here and now; She does not replace Him, but makes Him visible, demonstrates Him without being confounded with Him".[20]

The Ascended Christ who fulfils the offices of King, Priest and Prophet in himself, and through his Body the Church, is the Source of the Church's life on earth through the presence of the Holy Spirit. And since this gift emanates from the One who was dead, is alive for evermore, and is exalted to the heavenly places, it is inadequate to say that the Resurrection alone accounts for the existence of the Christian Church. The Ascension must also be included since "the Church as the Body of Christ is founded on faith in the exalted Christ who still intervenes in earthly events".[21] The Ascension accounts for the beginning of that story of the Church[22] which Luke is telling, "…this is what gives him his unique place in the New Testament. He is the Father of Church History".[23]

At the same time, while living within the limits of history, the Church always transcends such limits since she shares the life of the Spirit of the Ascended Lord who himself transcends history and time. Her members share, through the Spirit, "the power of an indestructible life" (Heb. 7:16) and they know that by virtue of their Ascended Head, victorious outcome is assured. "This Church is not yet the Church triumphant...if it suffers with Christ, it will *reign* with Him (11 Tim. 2:12), and of that the Church already has a glorious anticipation in its sufferings for Christ. Just as the New Testament speaks of Christ's humiliation, His uplifting, (*analēmpsis* Luke 9.51) on the Cross of shame, as already His exaltation in prelude to His Ascension to the throne above, (*hupsoun* John 3:14; 8:28; 12:33;34; Acts 2:33; 5:31)...through the Spirit, it is made to sit with Christ in heavenly places (Eph. 1:20; 2:6)".[24]

The Spirit interprets the mind of the Ascended Lord to his Church on earth (1. Cor. 2:16; Cf: John 13:26), ever recreating the life of her members, fashioning and forming them into the likeness of himself by providing the means of communication between earth and heaven, and by sharing[25] diverse gifts to his people, those for which they are best suited; "Therefore it is said, When he ascended on high he led a host of captives, and he gave gifts to men. ...And his gifts were that some should be apostles, some prophets, some evangelists, some pastors and teachers, for the equipment of the saints, for the work of ministry, for building up the body of Christ, until we all attain to the unity of the faith and of the knowledge of the Son of God, to mature manhood, to the measure of the stature of the fullness of Christ..." (Eph. 4:8f).

CHAPTER SIX

The Christian Hope

The New Testament makes it abundantly plain that Jesus stood in a unique relation to God the Father as the Beloved Son, (*Huios ho agapētos*), confirmation which was given especially at his Baptism (Matthew 3:17; Mark 1:11; Luke 3:22), and again at the Transfiguration (Matthew 17:5; Mark 9:7; Luke 9:36; Cf: 11 Peter 1:17). It is this latter event which, as Davies shows, anticipates both the Ascension and the Parousia,[1] that tells how

> "in Jesus Christ alone, both body and spirit were the perfect instrument of the Spirit of God; and some have supposed that Jesus Christ in His perfect manhood was able to pass to a heavenly glory without death, and have thought that the story of the Transfiguration suggests this. But He died because He made Himself utterly one with us and trod the road which our maimed and mortal manhood has to tread".[2]

If we examine the Scriptures to ascertain wherein the uniqueness of Jesus lies as the Son of God,[3] we discover that it is in his consciousness of doing always the Will of the Father[4] perfectly, which resulted in a life of total obedience even to the point of death.[5] This is the essence of the Philippian 'hymn' where Jesus is exalted as the consequence of his obedience unto death on the Cross[6] (Phil. 2:7f). And since his obedience is a perfect and complete offering of himself to the Father, not just his Spirit, but the matter of which his body was composed, this is seen as being included in his self-offering in so far as it is transformed and taken up by the recreating power of God "as being used and used up in the creation of the new life, as fuel is used up to produce energy...the physical...on that showing, is the good and purposeful work of the good Creator..."[7]. And further, because "obedience is the key to eternal life"[8], we see in Jesus the complete transformation and transition of his body of flesh and blood from the temporal to the eternal realm, from the earthly to the heavenly sphere.[9] The Resurrection alone cannot account for this, since Christ's risen self became visible in time and space and was in some sense realised 'on earth',[10], whereas the Ascension becomes the "'symbol' for the transition from the one to the other, as well as for the organic linking together of the two...first the conquest of death, then transition; first resurrection, then ascension: this seems to have been the expected succession of events".[11] Only so can we understand the Glorified Jesus to have entered heaven, the Unique, Eternal, Son of God returning to his Father.

THE ASCENSION OF THOSE WHO ARE IN CHRIST

The Incarnation was an act of Divine Grace for the salvation of the world, and the Death, Resurrection and Ascension of Jesus Christ, which involved him throughout, are seen as something done not for himself, but for the human race.[12] Already we have seen that the Ascension means the taking up of our humanity by the Son into the Presence of the Father, and that his identity with mankind – explicitly expressed through his frequent self-description, the Son of Man – makes possible the ascension of believers. If it be argued that this is to literalize what happens to the believer at death, the reply will necessarily be that what Christ has done once and for all in history, becomes an experience for the believer. Baptism is spoken of as a dying and rising with Christ (Romans 6:4f; Col. 2:12), and the life of the Christian as one of having "been raised with Christ" (Col. 3:1). Our identity with him should, therefore, not be any more difficult to accept in terms of his Ascension, that it is when it is expressed in our oneness with him in his Death and Resurrection. Rightly, the Apostle speaks of the believer as being "raised up with Christ and made to sit with him in the heavenly places in Christ Jesus" (Eph. 2:6), and spiritual experiences brought together here and now find their ultimate completion at the termination of the believer's earthly existence.[13]

Thus, the Ascension becomes the focal point of the Christian Hope, not to replace or supplant the Resurrection, but as the completion of the latter. As Flender so fittingly writes,

> *"The determinative cause of the future resurrection of the individual Christian is not the resurrection of Jesus himself but his exaltation. It is because Jesus has been exalted to the right hand of God that he can be leader or initiator of the Resurrection of the dead.* Jesus' Resurrection is here viewed from the angle of his new life with God in heaven...the Resurrection of Jesus is offered the individual as the eschatological message of new life in Christ, while the Exaltation is Jesus' entrance into the divine world".[14] (Italics mine)

Into that divine world he entered at the Ascension, to remain there until the Parousia, and, now at the Throne of the Godhead, the Ascended Christ as our Representative with our flesh, our human nature exalted in him to God, is the guarantee of our eventually ascending to heaven,[15] through the operation of the transforming power of the Holy Spirit in the life of the believer.

If it be asked, "When does this take place?", the reply must surely be, as far as the individual is concerned, "at the moment of physical death".[16] It is therefore, difficult here to follow the thought of Professor Oscar Cullmann who is of the opinion that those who have departed this life are in an unconscious state, asleep, until the Parousia.[17] Such a view would appear to contradict the continuity of the life eternal, which is of fundamental importance to the thought of the New Testament whereby it is not broken, but consummated at death.[18] And while the emphasis is upon the quality of this life rather than its duration, the term *aiōnion* also rendered 'everlasting' takes it out of the time series[19] since God himself is "from everlasting to everlasting" (Ps. 90:2). We are, of course, not denying that there is to be an ultimate reconciliation of all things together in Christ at the Parousia,[20] the completion of the process whereby "God may be everything to everyone" (1. Cor. 15:28 Moffatt), but this in no way denies that at physical death, the believer receives his spiritual body which has been anticipated in the Resurrection and Ascension of Christ himself.[21]

It is this emphasis of exchange which Moule makes in his most illuminating article, "St. Paul and Dualism" where he shows that in 1 Cor. 15, the Apostle looked for the addition of the spiritual body to the physical, but by the time he wrote 11 Cor. 5:1f, he realises that it will not be a matter of addition, but of exchange since the continuous surrender of the material body 'used up' in doing the Will of God is the process by which the spiritual body is coming continuously into existence. In this way, there would be no hiatus which Paul, as a Pharisee, would be unable to accept, since the concept of a disembodied state would be, for him, an impossibility. Instead of being found 'naked' (11 Cor. 5:3) at death, the *sōma psuchikon* would give way to the *sōma pneumatikon*.

Since "flesh and blood cannot inherit the kingdom of God, nor does the perishable inherit the imperishable" (1 Cor. 15:50), the Christian Hope rests in the *sōma* (body) and not the *sarx* (flesh) being raised in Christ, for *sōma* (body) represents personality, as against *sarx* (flesh) of which the body is composed, we find that this means

> "an entire person *sōma* dies, and the same person is raised to life. It is not the same form there is a radical transformation. He dies mortal and corruptible and is raised a glorious body: he dies animal and is raised spiritual. But always it is the same individual, just as the seed that is surrendered to the earth grows into a plant which is dramatically different, and yet continuous with the seed".[22]

We need to bear in mind throughout that it was because of Christ's perfect obedience that his flesh did not see corruption (Acts 2:31, cf: Ps 16:10), so that

> "what...through the wisdom of God was possible in that holy flesh which the Lord was, may not be possible for the most of us with our sin-soaked brain and spoiled nerve-tissue, so that the actual mode of normal human resurrection may be necessarily different from His, though ultimately conforming to the body of His glory".[23]

It is because of the uniqueness[24] of Jesus himself in his life of total loving obedience and surrender to the Father's purpose that we are to share in what the Father has done through him for us all.[25] And it is just at this point that the Apostle uses a most helpful analogy when he writes, "For we know that if the earthly tent we live in is destroyed, we have a building from God, a house not made with hands, eternal in the heavens...for while we are still in this tent...we would be further clothed, so that what is mortal may be swallowed up by life" (2 Cor. 5:1f). At first, Paul appears to be using two metaphors which do not easily go together, those of a tent and of clothing,[26] but this difficulty is resolved when we are aware that the Cilician hair-cloth, woven out of goat's fleece called "cilicium", was used, both for the making of clothes and tents, and therefore, adequately sufficed as one substance for the two uses. And it is surely seen to be most appropriate since it applies to what Christ has done for all mankind, in the corporate as well as in the individual sense, for the very reason that "we would be further clothed (*ependusasthai*) so that what is mortal may be swallowed up by life" (2 Cor. 5:4). Boldly we say, in the words of William Bright,

> "Look, Father, look on His anointed face,
> And only look on us as found in Him",[27]

and through faith we believe that we shall ascend to the Presence of his Glory[28] because "he who has prepared us for this very thing is God, who has given us the Spirit as a guarantee". (2 Cor. 5:5).[29]

In this chapter, we have sought to show that the Christian Hope necessarily includes, both the Resurrection and the Ascension of Jesus Christ, because they are seen to be the "two moments in the anticipation of the ultimate home-gathering of the whole people of God".[30]

CHAPTER SEVEN

The Final Glory

A study of the Ascension will necessarily include the Last Things, since the *Telos* (End) is referred to frequently throughout the New Testament, and the "faith which thus unites us with the ascended Lord is inseparable from hope by which we stretch out to the final consummation at Christ's Second Coming, for Christians believe, with Augustine, that the Head, who has entered into glory, will draw His members after Him".[1] Believing that the Ascended Lord has never left his people, but in his own words, is the ever present Christ (St. Matthew 28:20), the Scriptures clearly indicate that at the Parousia, he will manifest himself visibly at the end of the age.[2] And, although this is admittedly portrayed in different ways in the New Testament, and the delay, of what was thought would be an imminent return, gave rise to certain reinterpretations, the hope, even in the most realised eschatological teaching, was never brought entirely into the present.[3] There was the hope of another Coming when the Lord would appear in the full glory of his Exalted Manhood,[4] and, Dupont, citing the appearance to Paul on the Damascus Road – which he regards as being distinct from the post-resurrection appearances to the disciples – says, "In Gal. 1:12, 16, Paul speaks of this appearance as an 'apocalypse', a glorious manifestation in which Christ revealed himself to Paul in his state as Son of God, *such as will be his appearance at the end-time*".[5] (Italics mine).

In order to see the relation of the Ascension to the Final Glory, our approach will necessarily be from the standpoint of Luke, the sole narrator of the Ascension, and, at the same time, one

CA – E

who like ourselves, lived in an age which was not so dominated by the immediacy of the Second Coming as were the earlier New Testament Christians, and therefore, lived with facing the prospect of a seemingly indefinite future.[6] For Luke, the great emphasis lies upon the fact of the Exalted Lord who has both fulfilled Israel's history and inaugurated the New Age, and he sees the Parousia as the ultimate revelation of Christ's present heavenly reign. This is, at the present time, known only to those who have faith in the Exalted Lord, but does anticipate "the time of universal restoration" (Acts 3:21 N.E.B.), when he will be revealed to all. Appropriately, Flender writes, "The parousia is the manifestation on earth of the Lordship into which Jesus entered in heaven. For faith, this Lordship is already present, though invisible; at his visible return, faith is consummated in the redemption of the body. Luke 19:36; 21:28".[7] Meanwhile, the Ascension means the arrival of Jesus, triumphantly in glory in the heavenlies, his reappearance in that realm which was his before the Incarnation, and therefore, "the Ascension, as Luke sees it, is a kind of anticipation of the parousia in heaven".[8]

The approach which Flender makes is both helpful and important, for, as he himself comments, "The introduction of the exaltation motif does not mean a reduction of the eschatology, but its transformation".[9] For the Parousia is not to be seen as something which is only to come at the end of time, and therefore, isolated, but as something to be revealed which is already present, thereby showing the closest possible connection between the two. As he writes,

> "We fail to appreciate Luke's theological achievement if we think that all he did was to postpone the parousia to a later date and substitute the Exaltation instead of it...he transfers theological statements previously associated with the parousia to the exaltation. That which is heavenly in a future sense is also heavenly in a transcendent sense. This is how he keeps up the tension between the present and future in the eschatological realization of salvation, which the apostolic age expressed in terms of an immediate expectation".[10]

Further confirmation of this is seen in Luke's omission of the coming on the clouds of heaven at the trial scene of Jesus when he gives the reply of Jesus to the question if he is the Christ as simply, "But from now on (*apo tou nūn*) the Son of man shall be seated at the right hand of the power of God" (Luke 22:69), whereas the words omitted do occur in both Matthew 26:64 and Mark 14:62.[11] It is not that Luke is unaware of the Coming of the Son of man "in a cloud with power and great glory" (Luke 21:27; cf:18:8b; 17:24; 26:30) as these references alone show, but rather that his emphasis falls upon the present heavenly reign of Christ of which the Parousia will be the open manifestation. "The *nūn* v.69 clearly refers to the Son of Man's session ad dextram"[12] which is a continuing event holding together both Ascension and Parousia.

The contribution which Luke thus makes is extremely important in so far as he retains the personal element in his narrative account of the Ascension as given in both Gospel and the Acts, and, at the same time, by his emphasis upon the Exaltation and the continuing presence of the Ascended Lord through the Holy Spirit until the Parousia, gives personal meaning here and now to that presence which will visibly be made known at the Last Day.

A foretaste of the Final Glory was seen at the Transfiguration[13] of our Lord, which also anticipated the Ascension as well as the Parousia, and it is in the intervening period between Ascension and Parousia which Professor Torrance calls the "eschatological reserve in order to leave time for repentance and belief in the Gospel",[14] that the Ascended Christ comes to his people through the presence of the Spirit, making himself known to them, and giving encouragement and hope of his Coming again at the close of the age. Thus, the Ascension maintains the right balance between the Christ of history and the Lord of faith, and as "the ascension directs our gaze also to the *Parousia* (Acts 1:11)",[15] it avoids "His presence among His people (being) interpreted psychologically...(whereby) He will cease to be of cardinal importance".[16] The Exaltation of Jesus, as interpreted by his Ascension avoids an undue emphasis upon the present as though the End were of little or no significance on the one hand, and, on the other hand, it does not dismiss the present as being merely a waiting time for a future kingdom which is unrelated to the present dispensation. "Now, not yet, present and to come"[17] is the resounding theme of apostolic Christianity and the *kerygma* of those who lived in the faith of their ever-present Ascended Lord and Saviour.

The Ascension, revealing an Exalted Lord who is yet to come, known now only by faith, will at the Last Day, be seen by all

(Revelation 1:7). His Coming will mean the final subjugation of evil, the transformation and renewing of, not only the world, but the universe itself:[18] "According to his promise we wait for new heavens and a new earth in which righteousness dwells" (11 Peter 3:13; Romans 8:18f). And as the renewal of the created order is dependent upon the "revealing of the sons of God" (Romans 8:19), and that in turn includes "the redemption of our bodies" (Romans 8:23) then we may assume that at his Coming again, the Exalted Christ will appear to deal, not with sin, but with our perfection. As Cullmann[19] points out, this is not specifically mentioned, "but to save those who are eagerly waiting for him" (Hebrews 9:28), does suggest the final stage of our completion in him. For it is clearly stated that even now, "we all...are being changed into his likeness from one degree of glory to another; for this comes from the Lord who is the Spirit" (11 Cor. 3:18), and this surely means that as "God's children now...we know that when he appears we shall be like him, for we shall see him as he is" (1 John 3:2). Thus the Father's purpose as made known to us in his Son for those who are his brethren (Hebrews 2:11), will be seen to have been finally and completely fulfilled.

While *parousia* may be rendered by either 'presence' or 'coming' in most cases, though they are not always interchangeable as 1 Cor. 16:7 and 2. Cor. 7:6 show, we may nevertheless, think of the Final Manifestation of the Lord of Glory as the unveiling of the Ascended Lord and Saviour, the breaking through[20] of the reality of him who is now hidden from mortal sight, the One who "ascended...that he might fill all things" (Eph. 4:10). A most helpful analogy has been given by the late H. Burnaby which is well worth quoting here:

> "He is the Source from which the world draws all the light it has. He is its Sun. It is less true to think of the light of God in the world, than to think of the world as in the light of God – as the earth is in the light of the sun. The Christian belief in the Ascension is, therefore, belief that *Christ* is the Light of the world. Christians were led to that conviction by the experience of the power of Christ in their lives, of that gift of the Spirit which could come from no other source than from One who...'had ascended far above all the heavens, that he might fill all things'".[21]

Such an illustration helps us to understand that the presence of the Ascended Lord is no diffused spirituality or vague impersonal atmosphere, but the vital life and light of the glorified Person of the Ascended Christ beyond the reaches of the furthest human thought, and, at the same time, the One in whom "we live and move and have our being" (Acts 17:28). As Swete says,

> "The final Epiphany will not be such as to appeal to our present organs of sense; the descriptions which represent it as such cannot therefore, be interpreted literally. It may indeed be that the change which will pass over us will itself be the unveiling or epiphany or advent of the hidden Christ. He is hidden from us now through the grossness of our *body of humiliation*, at the moment when this is *conformed to the body of his glory*, the veil will be taken away, the eternal opened up to sight. In any case, the essential truth conveyed by the symbolic descriptions of the Advent is that a day is coming when the glory of Christ shall be revealed to all mankind".[22]

A contemporary writer, Dr. T. F. Glasson, similarly expresses the same thought when he writes,

> "What is to happen ultimately 'doth not yet appear', as it doth not yet appear what we shall be...our wisdom would be to hold that in a way beyond our understanding, events will move towards some consummation in which God shall be all in all, the present term of human life will be ended, the righteous judgement of God will be manifest, the children of God reunited in fellowship with one another and with their Lord".[23]

When the Church cries, "Come, Lord Jesus!" (Rev. 22:20), it is the prayer of those who "believe in the eschatological triumph of Christ...because they believe in the present reign of Christ"[24], because they who know him as Lord of their lives now confidently affirm that, in the Last Day, he is to be revealed as Lord of the earth, Ruler of the universe (Phil. 2:10f). So as Professor R. P. Martin says,

> "For the Church, it is a time of conflict and endurance of many enemies. But in the hymn (Phil. 2:5–11), the Church is caught up from earth to heaven, from the scene of conflict to the presence of the all-conquering Lord, from the harsh realities of what is to be the glorious prospect and promise of what will be because it is so already in God's sight. The hymn enables the Church to see beyond the present where Christ reigns invisibly and powerfully (but only known to faith), to that full proof of His reign in the heavenly sphere in which all powers are subject to Him and His dominion is manifestly confessed".[25]

Although the End (Telos) was expected to come soon as far as the majority of the New Testament authors were concerned, it is probable that for the Gentile author, Luke, it was anticipated a considerable time would elapse before the Final Consummation. His second volume, the Acts, portrays the spreading of the Gospel from Jerusalem to the Roman Empire and the hope of the Gentile world being brought under the Lordship of Christ.[26]

This is the period in which God has put his Church in the world. "For Barth this time which broke in with Jesus's ascension into heaven...in which the Church is united with Christ only in faith and by the Holy Spirit...is the interim time between His earthly existence and His return in glory...the time of great opportunity...of mission to the world".[27] And since "the Ascension is the beginning of this time of ours"[28] which is given to the people of God, our mission is to declare unhesitatingly an ever-present Lord and Saviour now, whose triumph is assured at the last, and One whose ultimate revelation will be manifest without and within; beyond and at hand, transcendent and imminent, the Jesus of history and the Christ of faith, the Lord of Glory with whom we shall for ever be (I Thess. 4:17).[29]

PART THREE

The Permanent Value of the Ascension for Christology

CHAPTER EIGHT

The Importance of the Ascension for Contemporary Belief

In our study of the Ascension, we have seen that while the narrative of the event is given by a single author in the Third Gospel and the Acts of the Apostles (the 'Marcan' account being later and almost certainly dependent upon Luke), the significance of the Ascension permeates much of the New Testament. Indeed, the whole of the New Testament witnesses to it since the writers take their standpoint from faith in an Exalted Lord, of which the Ascension is an integral part.[1] For Luke, the Ascension assumed particular importance as it is the only event which he records twice,[2] to show, on the one hand, the cessation of the post-resurrection appearances with disciples worshipping at the conclusion of his Gospel, and, on the other hand, declaring the opening of the history of the Apostolic Church through the gift of the Holy Spirit, sent forth by the Ascended Christ that the message of salvation might go to the ends of the earth (Luke 24:47; Acts 1:8).[3]

THE CENTRALITY OF CHRIST

The Ascension rightfully gives prominence to the centrality of Christ, both historically and theologically. There is a definite separation when Christ finally departs from this world, the time of faith,[4] and, according to Luke, after he ascends, another lapse of time,[5] a brief ten days, before the Holy Spirit is poured forth upon the assembled disciples in Jerusalem. As the Ascended

Lord and Christ, he stands above and beyond the world of time and space, and yet, his presence with the coming of the Spirit fills the universe (Eph. 4:10).[6]

RESURRECTION DEMANDS AN ASCENSION

If the Ascension is identified with the Resurrection as being one and the same event chronologically, even though it be distinguished theologically, and is therefore regarded as being without historical importance as an event,[7] there remains an inexplicable hiatus between the Resurrection and the Exaltation as to what did, in fact, happen to the Body of Jesus. The New Testament clearly asserts that at the Resurrection, his Body was transformed and glorified, and was therefore, no longer subject to the limitations of this world, except when he chose to reveal himself to touch and sight[8] for a period following the resurrection. Admittedly, he appears to be simply "the only visitor to Jerusalem who does not know the things that have happened there in these days" (Luke 24:18); and as the One who eats and drinks with them after he is risen from the dead (Luke 24:41; Acts 1:4; John 21:12; Acts 10:41). Yet his sudden disappearances themselves prove that, real and corporeal as he was (Luke 24:40; Matthew 28:9; John 20:20, 27), he immediately assumed a state of glory, a condition attained by the Resurrection (Rom. 1:4) to which the Ascension gave universal confirmation and expression in terms of his Exaltation. The Resurrection clearly demands an Ascension, not only to indicate that the post-resurrection appearances were being terminated, and that the disciples would no longer see him visibly as they had during the forty days, but even more importantly, to demonstrate that his going away would be no fading out, but his entry into glory. The Ascension remains the essential link between the Resurrection and the Exaltation; between the seen and the unseen; between earth and heaven, and without it, we are left with a question mark as to the nature of the finality of the Easter Appearances, the reason why they should then have ceased, or indeed, why they should have ceased at all. The Ascension is 'a point of transition';[9] the necessary complement of the Resurrection; the visible revelation of his Exaltation;[10] the continuity, under new conditions of "all that Jesus began to do and teach, until the day when he was taken up" (*anelēmphthē* Acts 1:1f).

KING, PRIEST AND PROPHET

Moreover, the Ascension shows Christ to be the fulfilment of the Old Testament offices of King, Priest and Prophet. As the King's Son, he sits at the Father's Right Hand, the seat of honour and dignity which is his sole prerogative, and the rejected Heir becomes the Chief Corner Stone.[11] As the Great High Priest, he ever intercedes for his people in heaven unceasingly, presenting them before the Father's presence, and as Prophet, through the mediation of the Holy Spirit, he is enabled to enter utterly and completely into the life of mankind[12] which was possible only in a limited measure during the Incarnation. The Man Christ Jesus, now exalted to the Throne of his Father becomes in his representative role, truly *the* Man of glory for all.

THE SPIRIT AND THE CHURCH

As the Risen Christ sends forth the Spirit,[13] the Church which is his Body is created, and he thereby presences himself in his Church so that the *plerōma*[14] is seen as being the "extensive movement spreading to the ends of the earth and the end of the ages".[15] While Conzelmann[16] makes the valid point that it is God who founds the Church, and not the Resurrection, it is, as he observes, the activity of the Spirit of God which accounts for the existence of the Church, and the Spirit is none other than the Holy Spirit sent forth by the Ascended Lord and Christ (Acts 2:33). It is therefore, inadequate to say, as is frequently stated, that the Resurrection can be held to account for the existence of the Christian Church; the Ascension equally plays its important part in the creation of the Church, the Body of Christ, and therefore, *both* the Resurrection and the Ascension make the Church a possibility, since the Gift of the Spirit comes from the hand of the Crucified who, by his being raised is now ascended into heaven (Acts 2:35–36). Conversely, it is often said that the Christian Church is the strongest evidence for the Resurrection, and, true as that statement is, it needs to be remembered that the existence of the Church is also the strongest evidence for the Ascension. The Christian Church gives testimony to the fact that Christ was raised from the dead, but did not remain on this earth; he ascended into heaven, and the fellowship of believers who constitute the Body of Christ are those who "do believe thy only-begotten Son our Lord Jesus Christ to have ascended into the heavens...also in heart and mind thither ascend, and with him continually dwell[17]", and with the Apostle declare that "God...made us alive together with Christ (by grace you have been saved), and raised us up with him, and made us sit with him in the heavenly places in Christ Jesus" (Eph. 2:4f).

PIONEER INTO HEAVEN

When Christ ascended to the heavenlies, "it was not man, but God in man who ascended",[18] and therein lies the hope of all believers. For he who has identified himself with mankind, the Son of God incarnate bore our humanity to heaven itself, and in the words of the great early Christian hymn, Te Deum Laudamus, "opened the Kingdom of heaven to all believers". As Dr. J. G. Davies points out, if Jesus had returned to earth after his Resurrection to restore fallen man to his pristine spiritual condition, this would have been occasion for great rejoicing, "but to enter with the second Adam into heaven itself is something which surpasses even that which the Resurrection by itself would have effected".[19] The fact that through his Ascension, he did enter heaven as the *Prodromos* Pioneer, "now to appear in the presence of God on our behalf" (Heb. 9:24, cf. John 14:2f), becomes the supreme blessing for man, and his anchor within the veil (Heb. 6:19). At death, he comes to his people in a new way, and yet they must await the time of his appearing at the end of the age *sunteleia*[20] for the completion and perfection of their being fashioned into his likeness. "When Christ who is our life appears, then you also will appear with him in glory" (Col. 3:4); "Beloved, we are God's children now; it does not yet appear what we shall be, but we know that when he appears we shall be like him, for we shall see him as he is. And every one who thus hopes in him purifies himself as he is pure" (1 John 3:2f). Again therefore, we see that the Christian Hope rests, not in the Resurrection alone, but in both the Resurrection and the Ascension, the two being complementary to each other, and, at the same time, both being interdependent. Because the Ascended Christ is now "seated at the right hand of God" (Col. 3:1), we are being prepared for eternal fellowship with him hereafter through his transforming power since "we all...are being changed into his likeness from one degree of glory to another; for this comes from the Lord who is the Spirit" (2 Cor. 3:18).[21]

CHRIST OUR CONTEMPORARY

Moreover the Ascension inaugurated the unseen life of Christ on earth until the Parousia, the latter, as we saw earlier, being anticipated by the former. As Swete appropriately remarks:

> "...how much remains of His work at which the Gospels hardly hint? His mediation and intercession, His high-priestly life of perpetual self-presentation, His reign, His exercise of universal authority, His certainty of complete victory, His gift of the Spirit, His Headship of the Church, His office of universal judge: – this is the contribution which is made by the second half of the New Testament to our knowledge of Christ. When all this is left out of sight, can we wonder that men do not get beyond a humanitarian view of His Person, and an equally defective conception of His Mission?...it is not strange that persons who take little interest in the heavenly life of Jesus Christ, regard the Church as a merely human society...nor is it matter for surprise that men of this type ignore the corporate life of the Church, contending that personal religion is sufficient for their spiritual needs".[22]

Swete puts his finger upon an emphasis which has to a great extent, been lost for several decades, and which, if it were to be renewed, would in all probability radically alter much present-day preaching, and the witness of the Church in the life of society. Maybe, it would turn current indifference into outright opposition, as in the early days of Christianity, but the Church's voice would once again be heard and noted, and for many would come alive in a new way, and in a convincing and convicting manner. The Jesus of history and the Christ of faith who is Head of the Church and Lord of all, would be known and experienced as the "Christ...indeed our Contemporary in whom we may trust".[23]

SUBJUGATOR OF EVIL POWERS

The Ascension puts Christ in his rightful place as being both Son of God and Son of Man, exalted at the Right Hand of the Father, with the powers of evil defeated and under his rule. Only to the eye of faith will he be seen as such, and often it will appear that evil is far from having been overcome in terms of suffering and tragedy of which we are all only too well aware today through the modern media of communication. But believers know that the victory of the Cross and the Resurrection, and the consequent bearing by the Ascended Christ of our humanity into heaven (cf: Heb. 9:24) is the guarantee that the ultimate defeat of all evil is assured. As Bultmann fittingly says,

> "Christ's ascent to heaven is simultaneously the act of subjugating the demonic world rulers...hence the whole cosmos... – heavenly, earth, subterranean beings – must pay homage to the exalted Lord (Phil. 2:10). Thereby, God has appointed an end for the cosmic disorder which originated in the primeval fall, and through him, has 'reconciled all things (i.e. the universe) to himself, as the Colossian 1:20 hymn says".[24]

Meanwhile the powers of evil have their day, and appear to control events as though they have the last word. But the Ascension proves otherwise to those with faith in the glorified Lord and Saviour, now exalted in heaven, for to use Cullmann's analogy, such powers are, as it were, tied to a rope, and therefore have only an imagined freedom. Sometimes the rope is shortened, sometimes lengthened, but it remains the rope by which those powers are held, thereby signifying the sealing of their ultimate doom.[25]

THE UNIQUENESS OF CHRIST

Probably the greatest challenge to the uniqueness of the Exalted Lord in our day will derive from an ever-increasing pluralist society with its search for a religious syncretism of the great world religions. Yet the Ascension reveals the Exalted Lord as being, not one among many of the great religious leaders, but "the only Son...of the Father" (John 1:18); "the Word...made flesh" (John 1:14); "the image of the invisible God...He is before all things, and in him all things hold together" (Col. 1:15); the Son of God who "reflects the glory of God and bears the very stamp of his nature, upholding the universe by the word of power" (Heb. 1:3); who "when he had made purification for our sins...sat down at the right hand of the Majesty on high, having become much superior to angels as the name he has obtained is more excellent than theirs" (Heb. 1:3b–4).

It was in 1928 at the World Missionary Conference in Jerusalem that Dr. J. R. Mott told how, after an exhaustive and comprehensive survey was carried through of all the great non-Christian faiths,

> "it was overwhelmingly proved that the more open-minded, honest, just and generous we were in dealing with the non-Christian faiths, the higher Christ loomed in His absolute uniqueness, sufficiency, supremacy, universality".[26]

Yet what may appear at first sight to be narrowly defined, *is* seen, in fact, to be both exclusive and all-inclusive. It is exclusive in so far that the Exalted Jesus can have no rival claim to his unique position as the Son of God in whom "all the fullness of God was pleased to dwell" (Col. 1:19). He is unique, adequate, indispensable and final as the Word made flesh, the one dwelling upon earth among men in whom the glory of the Father was made known (John 1:14). At the same time, the Exalted Lord is all-inclusive because he is, in himself, the very embodiment of the human race, the first principle of its existence,[27] the representative of mankind from its beginning to its end, "an event inclusive, but without parallel".[28] He is the Exalted, enthroned Lord in the heavenly sphere who is worshipped by

> "a great multitude which no man could number, from all tribes and people and tongues, from every nation, standing before the throne and before the Lamb...and crying with a loud voice, 'Salvation belongs to our God who sits upon the throne and to the Lamb'....saying 'Amen, Blessing and glory and wisdom and thanksgiving and honour and power and might be to our God for ever and ever! Amen,'" (Revelation 7:9f).

Salvation is through Christ Crucified, Risen, Glorified, Exalted , and there is salvation in no one else, for there is no other name under heaven given among men by which we must be saved" (Acts 4:12; Cf:John 14:6). It is "at the name of Jesus every knee should bow, in heaven and on earth and under the earth, and every tongue confess that Jesus Christ is Lord, to the glory of God the Father (Philippians 2:10f).[29]

UNITY OF EARTHLY AND HEAVENLY LIFE OF THE EXALTED LORD

To regard the Ascension story as if Luke were trying to dispose of the resuscitated physical body of Jesus, is to miss the whole point of the Ascension narrative. For as we have seen, the emphasis of Luke lies in the Exaltation of Jesus, which is demonstrated in the Ascension in his glorified Body. Yet it still remains true that whatever change had taken place in his person outwardly, some explanation had to be given that he was then entering into heaven as the Exalted Lord, and that his disciples would no longer see him in this world, but would meet him under new conditions in the place he had gone to prepare for them (cf: John 14:2f). Furthermore, the Ascension is seen as the climax, the focal point, the outward revelation "that here an ultimate and supreme thing comes into action, behind which there is no other reality...Christ is He who has *all* powers...if we believe".[30] At the Ascension, the Father's purpose, in and through his Son is attained, and the goal and destiny of man is reached. The Ascension is seen as that time concluding the forty days' appearances which can rightly be described as indicating the separation of the earthly and the heavenly life of Christ, and at the same time, the uniting of the two inseparably forever, since Incarnation, Crucifixion and the Resurrection demand it, and the Gift of the Spirit, the Heavenly Intercession and the Parousia are inexplicable apart from it. It is by his Incarnation that Christ has brought the life of heaven to this earth, and it is by his Ascension that he took in himself, as the Representative and Embodiment of the Human race, the life of earth to heaven,[31] thereby securing men's eternal redemption which he accomplished on the Cross in our world of space and time. That eternal unity which is the Father's purpose, known now only to faith, will be made plain to all when all things are made one, in and through the Ascended Lord – "For he (the Father) has made known to us in all wisdom and insight the mystery of his will, according to his purpose which he set forth in Christ as a plan for the fulness of time, to unite all things in him, things in heaven and things on earth" (Ephesians 1:9f).

THE ASCENSION TODAY

Far from being remote and abstruse, "the practical theology of the Ascension is the idealism of the Christian life",[32] and "men and women who dare to act upon this conclusion, and live as though Jesus were Master of all things, find the conclusion confirmed and substantiated by one experience after another".[33] It comes as a renewing call in our day to set forth the claims of the Ascended Christ who alone can allay the uncertainties and fears of this and every age, and as C. S. Mann has said, "What we need to recapture is the urgency of the apostolic proclamation of the Lordship. Rightly understood, the feast of the Ascension will compel us to take hold of that urgency".[34]

No alternative is required, no other answer to materialism, in whatever form it occurs, can adequately and finally show its insufficiency and prove that man is destined for "what no eye has seen, nor ear heard, nor the heart of man conceived, what God has prepared for those who love him"[35] (1 Cor. 2:9).

CHRIST ASCENDED – HISTORICAL EVENT AND ETERNAL STATUS

In the Ascended Christ, who at a point in history was taken up into glory and now reigns as Lord of all, there is to be found the basic answer to our quest for the meaning of life, here and hereafter, our relation to the universe of which we are all a part, and our relationship with our fellowbeings in the life and society of our day, full well knowing that we put our trust in him who is our Contemporary and our Eternal Lord and Saviour. Theologically and empirically, the Ascension of Jesus Christ is at the very heart of the New Testament.

Notes

INTRODUCTION

1. H. B. Swete, *The Ascended Christ*, (1916 p. viii). "I shall be thankful if these pages are permitted to set forward in any measure the revival of the great Ascension festival in parishes where the Church bell is silent or awakens a feeble response on the day when our Lord entered into His glory".
2. J. A. T. Robinson, *But that I can't believe!* 1967 p. 76f.
3. In I Cor. 15:7f, "Then he appeared...to all the apostles. Last of all...he appeared also to me", there seems to be a continuity without any distinction between the appearances to the disciples and the Apostle.
4. But see J. G. Davies, *He Ascended into Heaven*, (1958 p. 198) "...enough has been said to indicate that in all probability it was in existence at least from the first decades. It is this that both justifies and explains St. Augustine's declaration to Janarius (A.D. 400)...that the feast of the Ascension was of apostolic foundation or at least was instituted by an oecumenical council...".
5. A. Harnack, *The Acts of the Apostles*, (ET 1909 p. 155f.).
6. H. B. Swete, *The Apostles' Creed*, (1894 p. 64f.).
7. Davies, op.cit. passim.
8. U. E. Simon, *The Ascent to Heaven*, (1961).
9. T. F. Torrance, *Space, Time and Resurrection*, (1976).
10. C. K. Barrett, *Luke the historian in recent study*, (1960 p. 58). Cf: M. Dibelius, *Studies in Acts of Apostles*, (ET 1956 p. 123f.).
11. C. F. D. Moule, 'Expository Problems: The Ascension – Acts 1:9'. *Exp. T.* Vol. 68 No. 7 (April 1957, p. 205).
12. R. Bultmann, *Theology of the New Testament*, Vol. 1, (ET 1952 p. 45).
13. E. Schweizer, *Jesus*, (ET 1971 p. 4f.).
14. L. Hodgson, *And was made Man. An Introduction to the study of the Gospels*, (1928, p. 123). After a survey in which the author claims that here we are in the realm of deep mystery where we cannot be dogmatic, he concludes,

    "for my part, though I would be the first to deny any right to claim knowledge either of truth or falsehood of these miracles (i.e. the mode of His Birth or of His Resurrection)...whatever was the mode, it was a necessary mode...I am tending more and more to incline to the opinion that they did occur...the more I reflect upon the questions, the more that belief shows a tendency to ripen into conviction".

15. N. Clark, *Interpreting the Resurrection*, (1967 p. 91). Cf: A. Richardson, *An Introduction to the Theology of the New Testament*, (1958 p. 196), "It is exceedingly unlikely Paul would have countenanced any notion of Christ's Resurrection other than that of a physical resurrection in the sense of the narratives of the Empty Tomb".

CHAPTER ONE

1. C. S. C. Williams, *Alterations to the Text of the Synoptic Gospels and Acts*, (1951 p. 51). Cf: B. H. Streeter, *The Four Gospels; A Study of Origins*, (1927 p. 143), "It is the text which omits, not that which inserts, that has suffered harmonistic correction".
2. G. H. W. Lampe 'Luke' in *Peake's Commentary on the Bible*, (ed. M. Black and H. H. Rowley, 1962 p. 842f.), "Luke has probably felt it necessary to anticipate the narrative of Acts in this way by concluding his first volume with a summary statement of the event which forms its climax and is the turning point of the whole work". Cf: J. W. Packer, *The Acts of the Apostles* (1966 p. 23), "The cloud is more like the dropping of a curtain at the end of Scene 1 than an indication of the divine presence (cf: Ex. 19:9)". See also A. R. C. Leaney, *The Gospel According to St. Luke*, (1958 p. 295), "It is possible that the omission of these words was due to a desire not to anticipate the full account in Acts 1:9–11". Cf: P. A. van Stempvoort, 'The Interpretation of the Ascension in Luke and Acts', *S.N.T.S.* Vol. 5, (1958–9, p. 33), "Here Luke indicates the whole process of his passing away and being taken up in the wide sense".
3. H. Flender, St. Luke: *Theologian of Redemptive History*, ET (1967 p. 33), "Luke 9:51a embraces the end of His whole course of Crucifixion Death, Resurrection, Ascension, and not a single event of Ascension". He notes the similarity of δοξασθηναι J. Tinsley, *The Gospel according to St. Luke* (1965 p. 109) where he says that 9:51 is "more...than going to Jerusalem. It is already part of his ascension, when he was taken up to heaven". See also M. S. Enslin, The Ascension Story, *J.B.L.*, 47:1928 p. 61 ἀναλημψεως apparently refers to the coming ascension, not to his acceptance among men".
4. A. N. Wilder, 'Ancient Traditions of the Resurrection in Acts', *J.B.L.* Vol. 62 (1943 p. 311).
5. J. M. Creed, *The Gospel According to St. Luke* (1930, p. 302). Cf: C. F. Evans, *Resurrection and the New Testament*, (1970 p. 98), referring to Menoud's reconstruction of the text says, "The occasion for such a massive reconstruction of the text could have been when Luke's volume was divided into two to conform to the requirements of the canon. The first volume being now a work on its own included among the books called gospels, needed to be retouched to give it an ending which would make it complete in itself, and the second volume also now on its own, needed an introduction". Moule, op.cit., p. 206 believes Menoud's case for interpolation is not cogent on the literary level, and E. Haenchen, *The Acts of the Apostles*, (ET. 1971 p. 139) thinks it highly unlikely that Luke would have broken the already hardened mould of the Gospel in this way.
6. Moule, op.cit., (p. 207), "Is it not, then, simpler to postulate that Luke did alter his opinion about the chronology when he wrote Ac.1:3f, without harmonizing the story, than to assume an interpolator who deliberately

interpolates but has not the deliberateness to tidy up?" ibid. Cf: Enslin, op.cit., (p. 61), "On the whole, it does not seem a violence to feel that in the interim between Volumes I and II, the author has gained information of a kind that causes him to correct his chronology".

7. J. H. Ropes, *The Beginnings of Christianity – Part 1, Acts of Apostles 1925*, (p. 258).
8. Evans, op.cit., (p. 100), "There has been an increasing readiness in some quarters to accept the integrity, both of the longer text of Luke 24: 50–53 and of Acts 1:1–11". Cf: *The Holy Bible, New International Version*, (publ. G. B. 1979).
9 Haenchen, op.cit., p. 58; Cf: J. Jeremias, *The Eucharistic Words of Jesus*, (ET 1955, p. 99). "In most cases the longer version seems in all probability to be the original". Citing F. G. Kenyon, he observes that it is not only in the West that the pure text is to be found. Cf: Moule (op.cit., p. 205 n.1.), See also van Stemvoort op.cit., (p. 294), "the whole of my argument is a plea for the full text of B.C. and others. The shorter recension of the text is, in my opinion, the result of misunderstanding, harmonizing tendencies and lack of feeling for Luke's style". As Flender, op.cit., (p. 11) observes, Menoud, 'Pendant quarante jours' in *Neotestamentica et Patristica*, (1962 p. 148 n.1), has changed his mind from his earlier position and now accepts the Lucan original of both Luke 24:50f and Acts 1:1f.
10. Haenchen op.cit., (p. 138). Omit 51b and Acts 1:3 ἀνελήμφθη and a new main verb becomes necessary, otherwise the resulting text is meaningless. ἀναλήμφθη as a later edition found its way into every Greek MSS.
11. van Stempvoort (op.cit., p. 37). Cf: Evans, op.cit., (p. 101 n.), "It is doubtful, however, whether such a procedure is plausible, or that the two interpretations can be held to be complementary. At the least, if they exist they must imply a very considerable disjunction in Luke's mind between his first and second volumes".
12. D. P. Fuller, *Easter Faith and History*, (1965, p. 198).
13. Evans, op.cit., (p. 101).
14. Cf: W. G. Kümmel, *Introduction to the New Testament*, (ET 1965, p. 111), "Luke obviously pictured the Ascension in Luke 24 as the conclusion of Jesus' life, and in Acts, together with the forty days instruction and the message of the angel (1:11) as the beginning of the time of the Church" (Cf: Barrett, Haenchen, Meyer).
15. Hastings Rashdall, *Philosophy and Religion, Six Lectures delivered at Cambridge*, (1909, p. 165).
16. van Stempvoort, op.cit., (p. 34).
17. B. M. Metzger, *Historical and literary Studies, Pagan, Jewish and Christian*, (1968, p. 78). Cf: Haenchen, (op.cit., p. 58). "D it sy[cs] have omitted the words προσχυνησαντες αὐτον in verse 52. In their view with good reason: as soon as Jesus at the end of Luke was no longer understood to be taking final leave of the disciples, the expression for the behaviourism of the disciples corresponding to His final departure also lost its meaning and became superfluous". See also A. D. Martin, 'The Ascension of Christ', The *Expositor* Vol. 16 1918, (p. 326), "The great joy, too, with which the Eleven are said to have returned to Jerusalem after the parting would be incomprehensible if they had not witnessed something of further moment than another vanishing of Jesus out of their sight".
18. Metzger op.cit., p. 82, "It deserves to be mentioned that most of the numerals of Luke-Acts give the impression of being intended literally".
19. Cf: The Flood which lasted forty days, Moses was forty days and nights in

the mountain, Elijah fasted forty days, Ezra was not to be sought for forty days, the Children of Israel wandered for forty years in the wilderness, they were in subjection to the Philistines for forty years, David, Solomon, Joash, Eli all ruled for forty years, Ezekiel lay on his side for forty days, Goliath challenged Israel for forty days – these and several other instances indicate the significance of the figure forty. Cf: Swete, (op.cit., p. 68f.), As W. Barclay, *Crucified and Crowned*, (1961, p. 174) says,

> "The phrase 'forty days' simply means some considerable time. In the days of the early Church the Valentinians held that there were eighteen months between the Resurrection and the Ascension; the Ophites held that there were eleven or twelve years: Eusebius mentions the belief that the length of Jesus' ministry after the Resurrection was the same as the length of his ministry before the Resurrection. We may simply say that Jesus spent a considerable length of time with his disciples between his Resurrection and his Ascension".

Cf: van Stempvoort, op.cit., p. 39 "The number forty indicates that the appearances of Jesus Christ after Easter had a certain duration". Haenchen, op.cit., p. 353 observes that "the addition 'forty days' is also found in E C perp gig t sa Beg. III, 100 n.1.", and that Acts 13:31 "for many days" takes up Acts 1:3 ibid p. 410f. See also Torrance, *Space, Time and Resurrection*, (p. 83),

> "And so after Easter there is something like a history of the risen Jesus who came and went among the disciples, who spoke and ate and drank with them as he willed, in such a way that he could be touched and seen to be no apparition, but above all it was the *personal self-identification of the familiar Jesus* that was the paramount factor: that is surely the importance and yet the baffling nature of the forty days before Pentecost".

This appears to be a modification of his earlier view stated in Royal Priesthood, *SJT Occasional Papers* No. 3, (1955 p. 50) where he writes, "...there can be no historiography of the forty days of the resurrection, for the New Man breaks through the limitations of our crumbling time (Brunner's phrase) and does not come within what the secular historian as such with his methods and canons of credibility can establish as history". It is, of course, true that the new transcends the old order, and that eternity lies outside time as we know it in this present world; nevertheless, there did come a point when the Risen Christ was no longer visibly seen by His disciples, even in His glorified resurrection body.

20. Moule, op.cit., (p. 207). Cf; Evans, op.cit., (p. 112f.). See also Davies, op.cit., (p. 52 n.1). As Bultmann says, *Theology of the New Testament*, Vol. 1 (ET. 1952 p. 45), "The appearances of the Risen Lord probably were not confined to Galilee, but also occurred at Jerusalem after the disciples had returned there". See also A. M. Ramsey, *The Resurrection of Christ*, (1945 p. 71); Hodgson, op.cit., (p. 127f); H. E. W. Turner, 'Expository Problems, The Resurrection' in *Exp.T.* Volume 68 No. 12 (Sept. 1957, p. 370); N. Clark, *Interpreting the Resurrection*, (1967 p. 90).
21. Evans op.cit., (p. 98). Cf: Kümmel op.cit., (p. 109f.), "Acts 1:2 is hardly translatable".
22. Haenchen, op.cit., (p. 145).
23. C. K. Barrett, *Luke the Historian in Recent Study*, (1960 p. 55). "Luke is the only New Testament writer who makes any conscious attempt to show how, when the earthly life of Jesus was over, the Church came into being, and to relate the one to the other".
24. van Stempvoort, op.cit., (p. 37).
25. Moule, op.cit., (p. 207f.).

26. W. Milligan, *The Ascension and High Priesthood of Our Lord*, (1892, p. 4). Cf: G. H. Boobyer, *St. Mark and the Transfiguration Story*, (1942, p. 24f.). While the Resurrection Body of Jesus may not have been the shining body of δσξα as witnessed at the Transfiguration, it still remains true that it was not subject to the limitations of time and space, and therefore had supernatural features. Cf: B. W. Bacon, 'The Ascension in Luke and Acts', *The Expositor* Vol. 7, (1909, p. 258f.).
27. Cf: F. F. Bruce, *Commentary on the Book of Acts*, (1954, p. 40). See also H. Conzelmann, *An Outline of the Theology of the New Testament*, (ET. 1968, p. 67), "The appearances are thus regarded as appearances from heaven". Cf: P. Benoit, *Jesus and the Gospel*, Vol. 1. (ET. 1973, p. 246f.).
28. Although Paul does link his own conversion experience on the Damascus Road in 1 Cor. 15:8 with the post-resurrection appearances, the fact remains that his was distinctive and different since he saw no visible figure of the Risen and Glorified Lord, only "a light from heaven, brighter than the sun, shining round me and those who journeyed with me" (Ac. 26:13). Cf: H. Conzelmann, *The Theology of St. Luke*, ET. 1961, p. 203, "During the forty days, the appearances do not take place from Heaven. *Such appearances presuppose the Ascension and are of a different kind, for they establish no relationship with the Lord in the special sense that the Resurrection appearances do*. (Italics mine) An example of the 'appearances from Heaven' is given in the threefold account of the appearance near Damascus".
29. F. J. Foakes-Jackson, *The Acts of the Apostles*, (Moffatt Commentary, 1932, p. 2). "Latin versions favour 'eating together'. The fact must not be forgotten that the Risen Christ did eat – Mark 16:14; Luke 24:30, 41–2; John 21:9–12; Acts 10:41." Cf: F. F. Bruce, *Commentary on the Book of Acts*, (1954, p. 36), where he says that "eating" is preferable to "being assembled". In a note p. 30, Bruce thinks that "being assembled" is unlikely in view of the singular number and the present tense συναλι ζ ομενος . It is cognate with ἅλς (salt), and therefore means literally "eating salt with". He observes that the Risen Christ literally ate as stated in Acts 1:4, and that food was taken by him, not of necessity, but as proof that he was no phantom.
30. Barclay, op.cit., (p. 178).
31. C. F. D. Moule, 'St. Paul and Dualism, The Pauline Conception of Resurrection', *N.T.S.*, Vol. 12, (1966, p. 109), "the change is already anticipated, in so far as individual Christians begin to 'become' what they already 'are' in Christ (for Christ the change is already complete)".
32. J. H. Bernard, Ascension and Assumption', (1909, p. 155). Cf: Haenchen, op.cit., (p. 140), "ὀπτάνομαι means appear, show oneself, but *not* in the sense of vision...Luke does not regard the appearance of the risen Christ as visions!"
33. Barrett, op.cit., (p. 36).
34. Flender, op.cit., (p. 12).
35. B. H. Streeter, *The Four Gospels*, (1927, p. 408), "The words in Luke 24:51 which mention the Ascension as taking place *in sight of* the Twelve are probably original. In any case the Acts, by the same author, describes the event".
36. A. W. Argyle, 'The Ascension', *Exp.T.* Vol. 66, No. 8 (May 1955, p. 240).
37. Barclay, op.cit., (p. 176). Cf: Moule, 'The Ascension-Acts 1:9', *Exp.T.* Vol. 168, No. 7, 1957 (p. 208). "It is like an acted declaration of finality".
38. van Stempvoort, op.cit., (p. 38). Cf: Benoit, op.cit., (p. 246).

39. H. B. Swete, *The Apostles' Creed*, (1894, p. 174). "It is contrary to the usage of the New Testament to interpret ἐγειρεσθαι of any exaltation beyond the mere recall from death". Cf: Davies, op.cit., (p. 30f.), for a study of lexicography of the words 'rise' and 'ascend', and the distinction between them in meaning.
40. van Stempvoort, op.cit., (p. 38).
41. A. M. Ramsey, 'What was the Ascension'? *S.N.T.S.*, Bulletin 11 (1951, p. 50)., Cf: G. H. W. Lampe 'The Holy Spirit in the Writings of St. Luke', Studies in the Gospels 1955 ed. D. E. Nineham, (p. 177) where he states that "the apostles actually saw the Lord ascending".
42. A. M. Ramsey, 'Ascension' *A Theological Word Book of the Bible*, (ed. A. Richardson, 1951, p. 23.) Cf: C. S. C. Williams, *The Acts of the Apostles*, (1957).
43. Haenchen, op.cit., (p. 149).
44. Bruce, op.cit., (p. 41).
45. Metzger, op.cit., (p. 83). Cf: Evans, op.cit., (p. 141n.).
46. Cf: Metzger, ibid, (p. 84).

> "For if Jesus rose from the dead, not with a material, but with a spiritual (or glorified) body – and this is undoubtedly the teaching of the New Testament – then it would appear to be inappropriate for him to remain permanently on earth. The translation of his resurrected body to that sphere of existence to which it properly belonged can be said to be both natural and necessary".

Cf: J. Denney, (Ed. J. Hastings, *A Dictionary of the Bible, The Ascension*, 1898, p. 162),

> "To talk about Copernicanism in this connection, and to object to the whole idea of Ascension because we cannot put down the heaven into which Jesus entered on a star-map, is to misconceive the Resurrection and everything connected with it. The Lord of Glory manifested Himself to His own, and at last put a term to these manifestations in a mode as gracious as it was sublime; but the whole series of events is one with which astronomy has nothing to do".

See also Milligan, op.cit., (p. 26).

47. E. Stauffer, *New Testament Theology*, (1955, p. 138f.).
48. Haenchen, op.cit., (p. 146), "It is probable that the gospel first became canonical and only later (because Luke was one of the four evangelists), his second book also, Acts". ibid. Cf: Evans, op.cit., (p. 100) refers to the "dramatic shift that has taken place in Lucan studies, whereby Luke 'the historian' has had to yield to Luke 'the theologian of sacred history' "by citing Hugh Anderson in *The Easter Witness of the Evangelists, Essays in Memory of G. H. C. Macgregor* (1965 p. 49f), adds that "Luke would not have felt any contradiction in a forty days interval period in which the apostles were prepared for their task of witness". ibid. See also G. H. C. Macgregor, *The Interpreter's Bible*, Vol. 9, (1954, p. 434), "Probably Luke was not interested in matters of chronology when he wrote his first version of the incident. At any rate, he was not conscious of any discrepancy between the two accounts". Cf: Milligan, op.cit., (p. 340), "In any case there is no contradiction between the two accounts". Also note V. H. Stanton, 'The Synoptic Gospels' in *The Gospels as Historical Documents*, Part II, (1909, p. 309). As V. Taylor, 'The Passion Narrative of St. Luke', (ed. O. E. Evans), *S.N.T.S.*, 19, (1972, p. 115) comments, citing Stanton with approval, "The Narrative is the composition of the evangelist. He may be adapting a source, although this is not indicated by the diction".
49. Kümmel, op.cit., (p. 91), "Luke's goal in his work was to awaken...by

means of trustworthy reproduction of the narratives, complete trust in the contents of Christian teaching. Towards this end, he investigated, from the beginning, (ἄνωθεν) the divinely guided history, and strove for complete (πάσιν) and accurate (ἀκριβῶς) information, so that he could write an orderly account (καθεξῆς)".

50. Moule, op.cit., p. 209.

CHAPTER TWO

1. Cf: Bultmann, op.cit., (p. 45). "How the appearances enumerated in 1 Cor. 15:5–8 are to be distributed between Galilee and Jerusalem cannot be known, and it is mere supposition that the appearance to the five hundred brethren (1 Cor. 15:6) is identical with the event of Pentecost".
2. Cf: C. H. Dodd 'The appearances of the Risen Christ' *Studies in the Gospels* (ed. D. E. Nineham, 1955, p. 23) where he remarks that "1 Cor. 15:3–8 has not been 'written up', otherwise what a story we might have had of the appearance of Christ which was crucial for the whole history of the Church, but which had inexplicably failed to enter into the Gospels! The Gospels are far from covering the whole ground of the list given in the Pauline kerygma".
3. Since Bethany lay on the eastern slopes of Mount Olivet, there is no real discrepancy between the location in Luke 24:50 and Acts 1:12 as A. W. Argyle, *The Christ of the New Testament*, (1952, p. 146) points out; see also Moule, op.cit., (p. 206 n.6), "There is reason to believe that Bethany was on the Mount of Olives. See *The Beginnings of Christianity* v. 475f". Matthew's final scene is definitely in "Galilee...the mountain to which Jesus had directed them" (Matt. 28:16).
4. Cf: Moule op.cit., (p. 207), "Even the Matthean commission (Matthew 28:18–20) on a mountain in Galilee does not preclude a command to go up to Jerusalem for the forthcoming festival and start to implement the commission there".
5. Swete, op.cit., (p. 65).
6. Cf: Davies, op.cit., (p. 176) where he states that he believes this to be a post-Ascension scene, since the promise of the abiding presence of Christ with His followers continues to the end of the age, and only "in very few instances does this involve a visual presence". But there is everything in this instance to suppose that Christ was seen visibly by those who gathered with him on the Galilean mountain. As Evans, op.cit., (p. 83) comments, "It is an exaltation scene...there is nothing temporary about it...any subsequent movement from Galilee to Jerusalem would be unthinkable". But as Ramsey, 'What was the Ascension'?, *S.N.T.S.*, Bulletin II (1951, p. 49) points out, "It is conceivable that the concluding scene of the Gospel may be understood as a theophany in which Jesus, invested with divine authority and sovereign power, proclaims the universal and perpetual nature of his presence with the Church. If this is so, then it ends with ascension-glory manifestation, *but seems precarious*" (italics mine).
7. See A. M. Ramsey, *The Resurrection of Christ*, (1961 revised edition, p. 49ff) for "the line of writers from Strauss onwards, who have concluded that the appearances of Jesus recorded in the Gospels were simply visions generated by the imaginations of the disciples out of an intense state of emotion or expectancy. In a state of fervent devotion they imagined that they saw Jesus".
8. Kümmel, op.cit., (p. 71f.).

9. C. S. C. Williams, *Alterations to the Text of the Synoptic Gospels and Acts*, (1951, p. 44f.).
10. Kümmel, op.cit., (p. 72).
11. ibid.
12. W. R. Farmer, 'The Last Twelve Verses of Mark', *S.N.T.S.*, (1974, p. 109).
13. Davies, op.cit., (p. 43). Cf: Metzger, op.cit., (p. 79), "Though not part of the original form of the second Gospel, the long ending has been generally recognised by the Church as part of the canonical text of Mark".
14. Cf: John 16:16, "A little while, and you will see me no more; again, a little while, and you will see me". Commenting on this verse, C. K. Barrett in *Peake's Commentary on the Bible*, (ed. M. Black and H. H. Rowley, 1962, p. 863) says,

    "As it stands, this verse is, and was no doubt intended to be, ambiguous. It might, at first appear to refer to the events immediately in prospect: Jesus will after his crucifixion disappear into the tomb, and reappear on Easter Day. But it could equally be interpreted, and in the sequel many points suggest that it should be interpreted, of the removal of Jesus from bodily sight at the Ascension and his return at the Last Day".

15. ἀναβαίνω (ascend), 3:13, 6:62, 20:17, πορεύομαι (journey), 14:2, 14:28, 16:7, 16:28; ὑπάγω (go), 7:33, 8:14, 8:21, 13:3, 13:33, 14:4, 16:5, 16:17: μεταβαίνω (depart), 13:1. All four verbs are indicative of a movement from one sphere to another in the life of Jesus.
16. Add ὁ ὤν ἐν τῷ οὐρανῷ A θ f 1 f 13 579 p m latt sy [(c)p]: ζ;R[t]; Kilpatrick, British and Foreign Bible Society (Second Edition, p. 283). See also C. H. Dodd, The Interpretation of the Fourth Gospel, 1953, p. 258f, "On earth, He is still ὁ ὢυ εἰς τὸν κόλπον τοῦ πατρός (i.18; for His ἐξήγησις of the Father takes place in His earthly ministry", and then Dodd adds the following footnote, p. 259n, "Hence the reading ὁ ὢυ ἐν τῷ ουρανῷ (iii.13), gives at any rate a perfectly good sense. The authority of ℵ B is against it, but the support of Θ and *fam*, 1, the Curetonian Syriac, Old Latin and Bohairic versions, with a formidable array of patristic quotations, is not to be despised".
17. As C. K. Barrett, *The Gospel According to St. John*, (1955 p. 250) points out, the sentence is incomplete needing an apodosis, and that

    "Commentators generally have adopted two kinds of supplement. (I) If the condition is fulfilled the offence will be greater... (II) If the condition is fulfilled the offence will be diminished or removed...each of these two interpretations appears to contain elements of the full meaning (and) this becomes especially clear when it is recalled that the ascending (ἀναβαίνειν) of the Son of man means at once suffering and glory; he returns where he was before (cf: 1.1)...it is impossible to say why John has left this sentence incomplete. The hypothesis is attractive that he did so in order to leave room for the twofold interpretation which he seems to have intended; but this could have been done equally well if he had written τί οὖν ἐὰν ...".

18. Swete, *The Apostles' Creed*, (1894 p. 66).
19. A. R. C. Leaney, *The Gospel According to St. Luke*, (1958 p. 296). "John 20.17 reveals a conception of an Ascension as a return to the Father, typical of that Gospel".
20. Cf: W. Barclay, *Crucified and Crowned*, (1961 p. 178).
21. Ramsey, 'What was the Ascension'? *S.N.T.S.*, Bulletin II (1951 p. 48).
22. ibid. Cf: Dodd, op.cit., (p. 443), "It seems difficult to avoid the position that some change in reference to what is called ἀνάβασις is implied between xx.17 and xx.27". See also Davies, op.cit., (p. 51), "We conclude, therefore, that for St. John, the occasion of the Ascension was Easter Day".

23. Barrett, op.cit., (p. 470). Cf: F. F. Bruce, 'The Ascension in the Fourth Gospel', *Exp. T.*, (1938/39 p. 478) says, "The simplest (though not necessarily correct) is μὴ πτοόυ for μὴ μου ἅπτου in John 20:17 (see J. H. Bernard I.C.C.)".
24. Barrett, op.cit., p. 470f points out that "the ascension is not referred to again in John, and is not described in the realistic manner of Acts 1.9 (and perhaps Luke, if the words και ἀνεφέρετο εἰς τὸν οὐρανόν are read in 24.51). It is a matter of common belief in the New Testament that after his crucifixion Jesus took his place in glory at the Father's right hand, but only the author of Luke-Acts makes of this belief an observable incident".
25. G. H. C. Macgregor, The Growth of the Resurrection Faith, 1, (1939, p. 218), "Throughout the Fourth Gospel, with the exception of a few 'concessions' to the more popular and materialistic view-point, death, resurrection, ascension, the gift of the Spirit are, so to speak, almost 'telescoped' into one single moment of glorification".
26. Metzger, op.cit., (p. 79), "Whatever one may believe concerning the genuineness of these (6:62, 20:17) as sayings of Jesus, there can hardly be reasonable question that the tradition recorded in the opening chapters of Acts was before John's mind as he wrote these words". Cf: Barrett in *Peake's Commentary on the Bible*, (1962 p. 867)." In general, John does not draw a clear distinction between resurrection and ascension, but in the resurrection narratives, he is compelled by circumstances to do so, though not to the extent of providing, as Luke does, a separate Ascension narrative".
27. Barrett, *The Gospel According to St. John*, (1962, p. 470).
28. Barrett, op.cit., (p. 405), Cf: B. H. Streeter, *The Four Gospels*, (1927, p. 408), in referring to John 6:62, he writes, "It gains in point if we assume that the story of the Ascension was familiar to John's readers".
29. R. Bultmann, *Theology of the New Testament*, Vol. 1 (ET. 1952, p. 45). Cf: Harnack, op.cit., (p. 155), "St. Paul had no knowledge of it" (i.e. the Ascension).
30. C. F. D. Moule, 'ed The Significance of the Message of the Resurrection for Faith in Jesus Christ', *SBT* Second Series No. 8, 1968 p. 7f, "W. Künneth...is among those who believe that knowledge of the empty tomb is implied in the ἐτάφη of 1 Cor. 15.4. he quotes K. Bornhäuser with approval (*in Die gebeine der Toten* Guterloh, 1921) as saying: 'It should never have come to the point that in spite of the "he was buried"...the phrase "he was raised again the third day" was understood in any other way than as raising from the tomb". Cf: G. H. C. Macgregor, *The Growth of the Resurrection Faith, 1,* (1939, p. 280), "Jesus appears in His σωμα πνευματικον which is the σωμα ψυχικον changed, the latter can therefore, no longer rest in the tomb. If Paul fails to mention the empty tomb, it is not because he rejects the evidence, but because he does not see in it the most important proof". See also C. H. Dodd, in *A Companion to the Bible,* (ed. T. W. Manson, 1945, p. 388), "Some critics hold that the story of the Empty Tomb, which is not mentioned explicitly by Paul or in the summaries contained in the apostolic preaching in Acts, is a later addition; but there seems no good reason for separating it from the whole Passion narrative, which probably existed in tradition substantially complete before Mark wrote".
31. H. B. Swete, *The Apostles' Creed*, (1894, p. 67).
32. Ramsey, 'What was the Ascension'? *S.N.T.S.*, (1951, p. 45).
33. Moule, 'The Ascension – Acts 1:9', *Exp.T.* Vol. 68 No. 7 (April 1957, Bulletin II p. 209).

34. Cf: C. K. Barrett, *From First Adam to Last*, (1962, p. 71), "At the Resurrection, Christ came to be Son of God *in power*, whereas previously (during the ministry), he had been the Son of God *in weakness*".
35. Swete, op.cit., (p. 67), "The hope of a καταβασις postulates an antecedent ἀναβασις , without which it is inconceivable".
36. C. L. Mitton, *The Epistle to the Ephesians*, (1951, p. 204), "The fact that the Ascension in Ephesians shows affinities with Luke-Acts makes it post-Pauline. Whether Paul's failure to mention the Ascension means his ignorance of it we may never know, but Eph. 4:8–10 is much closer to Phil. 2:9–11 than Acts 1:9". Cf: R. P. Martin, *Carmen Christi*, (1967, p. 239)." ὑπερυψουν is generally taken to cover the Resurrection and Ascension. A parallel instance of this one term to cover the whole of Christ's triumph is in 1 Peter 3:18f, where 'made alive in the spirit' expresses the entire scope of His post-Resurrection ministry...full emphasis upon the Victory of Christ and His installation in the seat of power and might". Cf: Haenchen, (op.cit., p. 149n.). "Revelation 11:12 and 1 Thessalonians 4:17 are parallels of rising heavenwards". See also Swete, op.cit., p. 68n. "If in Ephesians 1:20 the sequence ἐγείρας ἀυτον ἐκ νεκρῶν και καθιτας should be seized upon by a zealous advocate of the new teaching as a clear insistence of the omission of the Ascension, he would presently find himself confronted by the appearance of the missing link in 4:10 ὁ ἀναβὰς ὑπεράνω πάντων τῶν οὐρανῶν ".
37. See P. N. Harrison, *The Problem of the Pastoral Epistles*, (1921, passim), for a thorough examination and investigation of the matter of authorship.
38. Cf: R. H. Gundry, 'The Form, Meaning and Background of the Hymn quoted in 1 Timothy 3:16' in *Apostolic History and the Gospel* (ed. W. Ward Gasque and R. P. Martin, 1970, p. 203), "By common consent 1 Tim. 3:16 contains a quotation from an early Christian hymn...", and again, p. 204, "'Taken up in glory' most naturally refers to the ascension rather than the consummation. Indeed ἀναλαμβάνω describes the ascension in Acts 1:2, 11, 22 (and Mark 16:19), and in view of these parallels the noun ἀναλημψις almost certainly refers to the ascension in Luke 9:51 (cf: 24:51)". The entire chapter is an illuminating discussion on the whole 'hymn'.
39. Moule, op.cit., (p. 208). As he notes, it was not only the beginning, but also the end of that particular sort of encounter, and was as decisive and final as was the Ascension for the disciples, since he distinguishes the Damascus road encounter from the subsequent 'trances' and 'visions'. ibid, (p. 208, n.4.). Cf: Swete, *The Appearances of Our Lord after the Passion*, (1915, p. 130f.),

    "The appearance on the Damascus Road was unique; it came to an unbeliever and turned him to faith. He classed it with the appearances of the forty days, for it was not purely an effect produced upon the mind; the light and sound which accompanied the inward visitation gave it a certain objectivity and a relation to the phenomenal world. It was the only vision which he regarded in the light of the evidence that could be produced if the Resurrection were denied; he never appeals in this way to visions received during an 'ecstasy' (Ac xxii.17ἐν ἐκστάσει)...it was, if we may believe his own account, supported by the testimony of his life, a fact external to himself by which he was convinced against his will and once for all...that sight and voice sufficed for all the years that followed".

    See also C. H. Dodd, *The Founder of Christianity*, (1971, p. 168), where referring to the appearances in 1 Cor. 15:3–7, he says, "This is not an appeal to any generalized 'Christian experience'. It refers to a particular series of occurrences, unique in character, unrepeatable, and confined to a limited period". Dodd adds in a footnote, p. 181 n.6, "When Paul claims (1 Corinthians 15.8) that he had himself 'seen the Lord', after all the others, he admits that this was something unexpected, exceptional, and abnormal, *an appendix to a series already closed*". (Italics mine).

40. Davies, op.cit., (p. 33).
41. ibid, (p. 34).
42. Cf: Moule, op.cit., (p. 209), "Christian thought, apparently following eyewitness traditions, did find itself driven at times, to analyse and distinguish these 'moments' (baptism, transfiguration, crucifixion, resurrection, ascension, session at God's right hand, giving of the Spirit, parousia) as successive component parts of a single whole". Cf: J. S. Stewart, *A Man in Christ*, (1954 edition p. 137), "Sentences like 'We preach Christ crucified' (1 Cor. 1:23), and 'I determined not to know anything among you, save Jesus Christ, and Him crucified' (1 Cor. 2:2), do not alter the fact that all through Paul's religion, there runs the overwhelming experience of a Christ at his right hand, a living Presence with whom he can commune, in whom he can confide, from whom he can draw all the daily guidance that he needs; and that all through his Gospel there sounds the trumpet note, 'Christ, being raised from the dead, dieth no more' (Romans 6:9)".
43. Davies, op.cit., (p. 44f.), "The author of the Epistle to the Hebrews is less concerned with testifying to the fact of the Ascension than with expounding its theological significance; yet, needless to say, the latter rests upon the former".
44. Ramsey, op.cit., (p. 46).
45. ibid. "The noteworthy fact is that there are numerous references to the ascension and only one reference to the resurrection (13:20), but it would be a wrong inference that the author was unmindful of the resurrection as an event".
46. Quoted by A. W. Argyle, 'The Ascension', *Exp.T.* Vol. 66, No. 8 (May 1955, p. 241), Justin (Dial 38).
47. Bultmann, *Theology of the New Testament*, Vol. 1, (ET. 1952, p. 175f.), "According to 1 Peter 3:22...Christ's ascent to heaven is simultaneously the act of subjugating the demonic world rulers'.
48. Ramsey, op.cit., (p. 46), "Here is a passage about which either case might fairly be argued. The resurrection and the going into heaven are not necessarily identical".
49. Davies, op.cit., (p. 45).
50. Cf: R. H. Preston and A. T. Hanson, *The Revelation of St. John the Divine*, Torch (1955, p. 92), "The Dragon is the devil, who attempts to destroy the Christ by the hands of Pilate and the rulers of the Jews. But Christ is snatched up to heaven (the Resurrection and the Ascension) and the Church escapes".
51. Milligan, op.cit., (p. 11).
52. ibid., (p. 13).
53. G. W. H. Lampe and D. M. MacKinnon, *The Resurrection*, (1966, p. 18f.).
54. Cf: Ramsey, op.cit., (p. 43f.). See also D. Whitaker, 'What Happened to the Body of Jesus'? A Speculation, *Exp.T.* Vol. 81 No. 10 (July 1970, p. 310) where he suggests that the disappearance of the Body was on account of τυμβυρχία (grave-robbing), since he believes that "Jesus rose spiritually not physically" (p. 309).
55. Moule, 'The Phenomenon of the New Testament', *S.B.T.* 1967, p. 42. Commenting on the statement of Neville Clark, *Interpreting the Resurrection*, (1967, p. 97f.), "For the resurrection of the body is not the

resurrection of flesh and blood, and the event of the Resurrection has nothing to do with the reanimation of a corpse." C. F. Evans, op.cit., (p. 130) says, "While the resurrection of Jesus is not simply the reanimation of a corpse, it cannot be ruled out that reanimation might have had some sort of connection with it". As Whitaker, op.cit., (p. 307) observes, Paul's use of 'first-fruits' "means 'first in time' without implying similarity of mode" (see Davies, op.cit., (p. 171f.), for an illuminating discussion on 'first-fruits'), and that Paul's saying that "flesh and blood cannot inherit the kingdom of God" (1. Cor. 15:50), "is here referring to sinful humanity: he need not necessarily have had Christ in mind at all", ibid.

56. H. E. W. Turner, 'Expository Problems, The Resurrection', *Exp.T.* Vol. 68 No. 12 (Sept. 1957, p. 371).
57. ibid.
58. Barrett, op.cit., (p. 472). As he writes, "John offers no explanation of this power, nor is it possible to supply one; though it is legitimate to compare Paul's doctrine of the spiritual body (1. Cor. 15:44)". ibid.
59. J. H. Bernard, Ascension and Assumption *Encyclopaedia of Religion and Ethics*, Vol. 2, (1909, p. 153).
60. *The Church Times*, (May 25th, 1973, p. 10).

CHAPTER THREE

1. H. Sasse, 'Jesus Christ the Lord, The Exalted', *Mysterium Christi*, (ed. G. K. A. Bell and D. A. Deissmann, 1930, p. 105).
2. P. Benoit, *Jesus and the Gospel*, Vol. 1, (ET., 1973, p. 231).
3. Swete, *The Ascended Christ*, (1916, p. 7). "The 'going up' of the Son of Man into heaven was also His 'being taken up'; the Ascension was an Assumption, and the words answer two complimentary aspects of the event. The one represents Jesus Christ as entering the Presence of the Father of His own will and right; the other lays emphasis upon the Father's act by which he was exalted as the reward of His obedience unto death (LXX ἀναβμσεται in Psalm 24:3; ἀνελημφθη in Kings 2:11)". Cf: Argyle, op.cit., p. 241, "It is important to observe that the noun 'ascension' nowhere occurs in the New Testament, which prefers to speak of a 'taking up' or 'assumption' (ἀνάλήμψις Luke 9:51; ἀναλαμβάνεσθαι Acts 1:2 11, 22:1 Tim. 3:16), and 'exaltation' (Ph. 2:9). As in regard to the Resurrection, the emphasis falls upon the initiative of the Father...who took Him up thereby fulfilling Scripture (Ps. 68:18, 110:1, 118:22–23)".
4. Benoit, op.cit., (p. 248). Cf: Davies, op.cit., (p. 110 n.1), where he observes that Jerome earlier took this view of the exaltation on Easter Day being followed by a visible Ascension forty days later, and writes, "This is unconvincing because Luke, and the other New Testament writers, quite evidently regarded the Ascension as the occasion of Christ's entry into glory". It is not beyond the bounds of possibility that the two men in white robes (Acts 1:10) were Moses and Elijah in view of the close connection between the Transfiguration and the Ascension, the former anticipating the latter.
5. Cf: J. Denney, op.cit., (p. 161f.), "When faith in the Resurrection was assured in the apostles' hearts...He parted from them for the last time in such a way that they knew it was the last; He passed with something like kingly state to the right hand of the Father".

6. Metzger, op.cit., (p. 81).
7. Cullmann, *The Christology of the New Testament*, (ET. 1959, p. 88).
8. ibid (p. 222f.), "Scholars do not usually attribute sufficient importance to the fact that statements about the exaltation of Christ to the right hand of God (very early included in the Creed), formally go back to this Psalm. It is quoted throughout the New Testament, Rom. 8:34, 1 Cor. 15:25, Col, 3:1, Eph. 1:20, Heb. 1:3, 10:12f, 8:1, 1 Peter 3:22, Acts 2:34f, 5:31, 7:55, Rev. 3:21, Matt. 22:44, 26:64, Mark 12:36, 14:62, 16:19, Luke 20:42f, Matt. 22:69".
9. ibid, (p. 223).
10. Argyle, *The Christ of the New Testament*, (1952, p. 155).
11. Davies, op.cit., (p. 19). The existence, nature and possible significance of such a festival remain matters of scholarly conjecture.
12. ibid, (p. 19f.)
13. ibid, (p. 23).
14. Cf: J. Burnaby, 'The Ascension', *Exp.T.* Vol. 70 No. 7 (April, 1959), Review of Davies' Bampton Lectures, op.cit., under 'Literature', p. 203, "In general, the New Testament regards the Ascension as a *Christological* event". Cf: H. Roberts, *Jesus and the Kingdom of God*, (1955, p. 80), "We never cease to call Him 'Lord' even when we are permitted to know Him as a friend. He is other than we are, and, in spite of the ultimate union that is experienced, the gulf between Christ and those who are in Him remains. In the experience of faith-union, Christ is transcendent and imminent, and His dealings with those who respond to His call are fully personal". Cf: A. M. Ramsey, *The Glory of God and the Transfiguration of Christ*, (1949, p. 151), "Man...when he is raised up with Christ in glory, will be man as God created him to become – both *in his likeness to his Maker* and *in his utter dependence upon him*". (Italics mine).
15. Cf: H. Burnaby, *Thinking Through the Creed*, (1961, p. 52f.), "The two beliefs (i.e. Resurrection and Ascension) are complementary: you cannot believe in one without the other. But of the two, the Ascension is the more fundamental". See also Argyle, op.cit., (p. 153), "The whole of the New Testament after the Gospels presupposes the Exaltation of our Lord and is a witness to it. Indeed the Gospels themselves would not have been written but for it. The Christ of the New Testament is not merely the Jesus of history, but the Eternal Son of God, who has returned to heaven where He ever lives and reigns...the Christ whom the Apostles preached was the Exalted Lord, seated upon the Throne of God Himself".
16. Cf: Moule, 'Further Reflections on Philippians 2:5–11' *Apostolic History and the Gospel, Biblical and Historical Essays presented to F. F. Bruce*, (ed. W. Ward Gasque and R. P. Martin 1970, p. 271f.). See also L. P. Trudinger, ἁρπαγμός and the Christological Significance of the Ascension, *Exp.T.* Vol. 79, No. 9, (June, 1968, p. 279).
17. Cullmann, op.cit., (p. 224).
18. Cf: Cullmann, op.cit., (p. 180), H. B. Swete, op.cit., (p. 19) observes that Paul appears to use 'Lord' rather than 'King' to avoid giving offence to the Emperor, but by the time of the writing of the Book of the Revelation of St. John when there is open opposition to the Roman Empire, Christ is boldly referred to as being, 'King of kings and Lord of lords' (Revelation 19:16). Cf: V. Taylor, *The Person of Christ in New Testament Teaching*, (1958, p. 72f.).
19. Cf: Cullmann, op.cit., (p. 180), "This is not to say that only now is Jesus exalted to deity. Philippians is not adoptionism – 2:6 shows He is already divine in pre-existence. Already then he was the highest possible being in

his relationship with God...but now, because of his obedience, complete equality with God in the exercise of divine sovereignty is added...although he was already υἱός , now he becomes Romans 1:4 ἐν δυνάμις . Acts 2:3 expresses it 'made' '*Kyrios*'". Cf: Lampe in *Peake's Commentary*, ed. M. Black and H. H. Rowley, 1962 p. 822, "As Messiah, he stands in a unique relationship to God. He is 'Lord' from before his birth (1:43). Yet all this is proleptic. The infancy stories announce that Jesus is, and yet at the same time, what he is to become when through death he enters into his glory and is made (Acts 2:36) the Lord and Christ which he was proclaimed to be in the beginning". Cf: R. H. Fuller, *The Foundations of New Testament Christology*, (1965 p. 230), "The name granted to him at the exaltation was perhaps the name he had already possessed in his pre-existent state of equality with God. The difference is that it is *Jesus* who now has this name. God's Lordship is now effectively asserted in Jesus' history, and made manifest to the powers so that they acknowledge it. If this be so, then the pre-existent was already *Kyrios*".

20. R. P. Martin, op.cit., (p. 273).
21. Cullmann, op.cit., (p. 236f.).
22. Martin, op.cit., (p. 268).
23. Metzger, op.cit., (p. 87).
24. Barth, *Dogmatics in Outline*, (ET 1966 p. 124).
25. Cf: E. Stauffer, *New Testament Theology*, (ET 1955 p. 139), "But who is it that stands on the left of God's throne? It is Christ's counterpart, Satan, who accuses us before God...but Christ has the last word – that much is certain to the whole New Testament (Cf: John 12:13f)".
26. Barrett, *Luke the historian in recent study*, (A. S. Peake Memorial Lecture No. 6, 1960 p. 58f.).
27. Cf: S. Mowinckel, *He that Cometh*, (ET 1956 p. 446f.).
28. W. K. Lowther Clarke, 'The Clouds of Heaven. An Eschatological Study', *Theology*, Vol. 31, (1935, p. 131).
29. Cf: T. F. Glasson, *The Second Advent*, (1945, p. 65), who says that the fact of Matthew and Luke using different Greek words for 'From now' rules out a harmonious gloss and is proof of this being a genuine utterance of Christ.
30. J. A. T. Robinson, 'Expository Problems, The Second Coming-Mark xiv. 62' *Exp.T.* Vol. 67 No. 11 (August 1956), p. 338f.
31. Glasson, op.cit., (p. 64). Cf: Moule, *The Phenomenon of the New Testament* (SBT, 1968 second impression, p. 87f.), "But I am inclined, myself, to think that when the New Testament writers alluded to the Danielic clouds, they were in any case more interested in the exaltation, the glorification, of the Son of Man than in his ascending or descending as such...broadly ἀνάστασις, ἀναβαίνείν ὑψωθῆναι, δοξασθῆναι and μετὰ τῶν νεφελῶν all shared, as their primary association, the idea *vindication*, whether or not there was a secondary eschatological reference". Note in passing N. Perrin, 'Mark 14:62 The End Product of a Christian Pesher Tradition'? *SNTS*, Vol 12, No. 2 (1966, p. 151) that Daniel 7:13 in Jewish midrashic tradition is interpreted messianically in two different ways (a) As Messiah going to God from earth, (Pss. 2:9 and 21:5); (b) As Messiah coming to earth from God, (Genesis 13:11 and Numbers 13:14); Cf: Kümmel, *Promise and Fulfilment*, S.B.T., E.T. 1961.
32. Cullmann, op.cit,(p. 120).
33. Mowinckel, op.cit., (p. 450). He says that "this paradox must go back to Jesus Himself, which finds expression in the daring way in which He transforms and uses the concept of Son of Man". ibid. Cf: Cullmann,

op.cit., (p. 161), "Jesus united Son of Man and Servant as it declares both his humiliation and his exaltation. He prefers the former to the latter because it is more comprehensive".

34. Moule, op.cit., (p. 89).
35. ibid (34f.).
36. Dodd, op.cit., (p. 244). Cf: Moule, op.cit., (p. 93), "The new humanity, the saints, the sons of God-whatever terms St. Paul uses to describe those who are in Christ-have been vindicated by the death and resurrection of the one who was seen in human form (σχήματι εὑρεθεὶς ὡς ἄνθρωπος) and has been very highly exalted". The phrase Son of Man is found twice only outside the Gospels in Acts 7:56 and Rev. 1:13.
37. Cf: A. J. Tait, *The Heavenly Session of Our Lord*, (1912, p. 13f.),

> "St. Paul has in view the spiritual union of Christ and the believer. It is true that the Resurrection and the Session of Christ are types of spiritual life, and anticipations of the believer's destiny, but they are not that alone...for him who has become one spirit with Christ, there is already a realization, in part, of heavenly session with Christ which is the earnest of the glory which is to be hereafter. The Kingdom of God is even now with us, eternal life is even now our possession, *the heavenly places* are even now our abode...the life of *the heavenly places* must be exhibited in those who claim to be seated there with Christ".

T. F. Torrance, Space, Time and Resurrection, 1976 p. 136 gives us a salutary reminder that

> "a warning should be given at this point on the danger of *vertigo* that quickly overwhelms some people when they think of themselves as being exalted in Christ to partake of the divine nature...the hypostatic union of the divine and human natures in Jesus preserves the human and creaturely being he took from us, and it is in and through our sharing in that human and creaturely being, sanctified and blessed in him, that we share in the life of God while remaining what we were made to be , men and not gods".

CHAPTER FOUR

1. A. Richardson, 'The Gospel in the New Testament', *The Enduring Gospel*, (S.C.M., 1950, p. 49).
2. Cullmann, op.cit., (p. 232), "After Jesus has left earth and ascended to heaven, he will not abandon earth. On the contrary...his action on earth will then be much more effective than it was during the time of the incarnation".
3. Bernard, op.cit., (p. 157), "The higher and more spiritual function of a priest is to *intercede*, Cf: Epistle to Hebrews 7:25, 4:14, 7:26, 8:1, 7:24".
4. Cullmann, op.cit., (p. 193f.). Cf: ibid (p. 106), "Jesus as Leader and Forerunner in Hebrews developed in John – He goes before his people and thus continues his high priestly office of mediation in the present".
5. Milligan, (op.cit., p. 34f.). Cf: Davies, op.cit., (p. 180f.), "The Ascension was not the exaltation of an individual man, but of human nature. It was therefore a unique event...it was not man, but God in man who ascended...it is the manhood of Christ, which has entered heaven through the Ascension, that provides the point of contact between God and us in our creaturely state".
6. Bernard, op.cit., (p. 157).
7. Argyle, *The Christ of the New Testament*, (1952, p. 151).
8. From the author's notes as a theological student when attending lectures by Professor A. M. Ramsey (now Lord Ramsey, former Archbishop of

Canterbury), on The Christian Doctrine of Redemption, in the Divinity School, Cambridge, during Michaelmas and Lent Terms, 1951–2.
9. Swete, *The Ascended Christ*, (1916, p. 43).
10. Milligan, op.cit., (p. 152f.).
11. H. Conzelmann, *The Theology of St. Luke*, (ET 1961, p. 178).
12. Swete, op.cit., (p. 45).
13. *The Baptist Hymn Book* (1962). Hymn No. 178 verses 2 and 3.
14. Swete, op.cit., (p. 49f.).
15. Cf: Cullmann, op.cit., (p. 102f.),

"The living Christ who intercedes for us now can do so only because he is the same Christ who was on earth, man, tempted as we are. Only for that reason, too, can he today sympathize with each individual. The necessity of his being man is thus related, not only to his unique act of sacrifice, but also to his present intercession for us. The idea that Christ intercedes for us also in the present is Christologically very important and ought to be given a more central place also in systematic theology than is usually the case. It is not isolated to Hebrews in the New Testament, but is one characteristic of Paul, and even more in the farewell discourses of John".

CHAPTER FIVE

1. L. Dewar, *The Holy Spirit and Modern Thought*, (1959, p. 14).
2. Referring to John 12:32, Dodd, op.cit., p. 375f writes, "In primitive Christian usage...the term ὑψωθῆναι was used for Christ's exaltation 'at the right hand of God'; and we must suppose the Fourth Evangelist to have this usage well in mind. In iii.14 ὑψωθῆναι would naturally be taken as an equivalent of ἀναβαίνειν, which appears in the context". In an interesting footnote, ibid, Dodd comments,

"it is to be noted that ὕψωσις ὕψωμα, *exaltatio*, were used in astronomy and astrology, denoting either the maximum apparent elevation of a heavenly body, or the date at which it exerts its maximum influence: see Moulton and Milligan, *svv.* ὑψόω, ὕψωμα. In the calendar of Asia, it appeared the festival of Ὕψωμα Ἡλίου was celebrated on April 12. It is a curious reflection that our evangelist and his fellow-Christians at Ephesus would be celebrating the death and resurrection of Christ just about the time when their pagan neighbours were celebrating the *Exaltatio Solis*. Since Christ is the Light of the World, it is not beyond possibility that this astronomical or astrological usage has helped towards the use of ὑψωθῆναι in a highly mysterious and significant way in this gospel. See G. Weinstock. 'A New Greek Calendar and Festivals of the Sun' in *J.R.S.* vol. No. 38 (1948, pp. 38–9)".

3. A. Richardson, *An Introduction to the Theology of the New Testament*, (1958, p. 116f.).
4. Cf: ibid, (p. 118f.),

"Luke's story conveys profound Christian truth, but the truth behind the story, namely, that after the Exaltation of Christ the pouring out of the Holy Spirit from on high took place, is plain historical truth, *although Acts 2 is not a literally true story*; the literal truth of 'what happened' is not recoverable by us, because the biblical writers, even St. Luke, are not chroniclers of the literal. Events transcended the normal and could not be recounted in human words at all, and yet they are communicable in the wordless language of Christian experience of the Holy Spirit". (Italics mine).

If this were the case, the claim by Luke to have "followed all things closely for some time past, to write an orderly account for you...that you may know the truth concerning the things of which you have been informed" (Luke 1:3f) would hardly apply to Luke's second volume of his work, the Acts, which seems unlikely. Cf: Moule, 'Expository Problems, The

Ascension-Acts, i.9' *Exp.T.* Vol. 68 No. 7, (April, 1957, p. 207), "Luke is, after all, the self-confessed *narrator* of the New Testament, (Luke 1:1f)". See also Flender, op.cit., (p. 139), "Acts 1:1f shows two distinct events, and they do not coincide as the Resurrection and the Holy Spirit in John 20:19f. The exaltation of Christ and the outpouring of the Holy Spirit stand side by side, but *they are separated in time and place*". (Italics mine).

5. Ramsey, *The Resurrection of Christ*, (1961, p. 89). Cf: Dewar, op.cit., (p. 39), who points out that "Westcott...argued in favour of a distinction between receiving a gift of the Spirit (without the article), and receiving the Spirit Himself (with the article". Milligan, op.cit., (p. 205) elaborates this further when he says, "'*The* Holy Spirit' refers to the Spirit Himself, in His personality, in the place occupied by Him in the Godhead; while the words, 'Holy Spirit' lead to the thought of His operation, and more particularly to His operation as manifested in its full power and magnitude in the Christian age".
6. Migne P. G. lxvi, 783, quoted by Swete, *The Appearances of Our Lord after the Passion* (1915, p. 34) (accipite pro "accipietis" dicit). Cf: Dewar, op.cit., (p. 40) who says that the most probable solution is to say, with Swete, that this incident is to be interpreted proleptically.
7. Swete, ibid (p. 35).
8. R. Newton Flew, *Jesus and His Church*, (1938, p. 145).
9. Cf: Dodd, op.cit., (p. 442), "Although it is declared that at the moment of the death of Jesus on the Cross all is accomplished, and that the life-giving stream, which is the Spirit (vii.38) is now released (xix.34) for the salvation of man, it is yet necessary that the Spirit should be given by the risen Lord to His disciples (xx.22). *Sub specie aeternitatis*, all is fulfilled in Christ's one complete self-oblation". See also Davies, op.cit., (p. 64, n. 7) where he draws attention to the fact that acceptance of the Johannine chronology forbids any identification of the Resurrection and the Ascension.
10. Milligan, op.cit., (p. 159). Cf: Cullmann, op.cit., (p. 106f.),

> "It seems to me that the concept of the Paraclete is especially related to the High Priestly concept – judicial, mediatorial. According to the application of Ps. 110:1 to Christ, Jesus continues to work in the present from the right hand of God; according to John he comes to earth in the Paraclete for his own. It is his highest high priestly function that he will pray to the Father and give you another Comforter to be with you for ever. This Comforter fulfils on earth the mediation of sanctification. He is the 'Spirit whom the world cannot receive' who will lead those who belong to Christ into all truth. On the other hand, the command to the disciples...to pray in Jesus' Name shows that Christ continues his high priestly work after his ascension by bringing their prayers before God in heaven. This is what is meant when Christians end διὰ 'Iησου Xριστοῦ".

11. S. Cave, *The Doctrines of the Christian Faith*, (1952, Third Impression, p. 221). Cf: Richardson, op.cit., (p. 121), "After the Resurrection...the New Testament writers do not attempt to distinguish between the operation of the Risen Christ and the operation of the Holy Spirit. Christ Himself comes in the coming of the Spirit...the Church is actually shaped and guided by the Spirit of the Risen Christ". See also Torrance, *Royal Priesthood* S.J.T. Occasional Papers No. 3 (1955, p. 25). "We recall that the doctrine of the Spirit has Christology for its content (John 14:17, 26; 15:26; 16:13f) so that the doctrine of the Spirit is really Christology (cf: 'the Spirit of Christ' Gals. 4:6, Romans 8:9, Phil. 1:19, 1 Peter 1:11) applied to the Church as the Body of Christ". Cf: Stewart, op.cit., (p. 156), "It is...natural and legitimate to use the phrase 'in the Spirit' to elucidate the harder phrase 'in Christ'. To say this is not to agree with Weiss (Das Urchristentum, 356)

when he declares that Christ and the Spirit are simply identified. The New Testament doctrine is that it is the Spirit who makes Christ real to us and mediates Christ's gifts to us: and this is not 'identity'". ibid. Note also E. F. Scott, *The Epistle to the Ephesians*, (Moffatt Commentary, 1952 Eighth Impression, p. 195), "It is often difficult in Paul's thought to distinguish between the Spirit and the indwelling Christ. Probably he himself was not conscious of any clear distinction. For earlier Christian belief, Christ was the Lord enthroned in heaven, and Paul also conceives of him in this manner. But with this mystical turn of mind, he also thinks of him as an inward, abiding presence, and his conception of Christ thus tends to fuse itself with that of the Spirit". Cf: Sasse, op.cit., (p. 117). See also Flender, op.cit., (p. 135), "For Luke, the present Lord and the gift of the Holy Spirit are parallel, but independent and complimentary in operation". Similarly, V. Taylor, *The Person of Christ in New Testament Teaching*, 1958, (p. 54) writes, "In Paul's teaching, the relationship between Christ and the Spirit is not one of identity, but is singularly close in range and function". Cf: also J. D. G. Dunn, 'Spirit and Kingdom', *Exp.T.* Vol. 82 No. 2 (Nov. 1970, p. 36f.).

12. Milligan, op.cit., (p. 194). Cf: Schleiermacher, *Glaubenslehre*, 124, 2, "The fruits of the Spirit are the virtues of Christ", quoted by H. Wheeler Robinson in *The Christian Experience of the Holy Spirit*, (reprinted 1952 p. 33).
13. Ramsey, *The Glory of God and the Transfiguration of Christ*, (1949, p. 151). Cf: Milligan, op.cit., (p. 196), "Christianity is always the impartation of a new life in Christ, not the improvement of an old life".
14. Cf: Moule, *The Birth of the New Testament*, (1962, p. 97), "When...he was finally and decisively withdrawn from sight, they looked forward to a very speedy return. And the vivid manifestation of power and confidence at Pentecost was hailed as an interim gift from the Exalted Lord, until the consummation of God's plan, when Jesus would return (Acts. 2:33, 3:21)".
15. Cf: Torrance, op.cit., (p. 35), "It is never applied in the singular to believers, only to Christ Himself".
16. Cf: Sasse, op.cit., (p. 112), "The Exalted Lord and His Church belong to each other...in such a way that it is impossible to think of one without, at the same time, the other...they belong to each other as the Head to the Body; the Corner Stone to the House; the Stem to the Vine".
17. Torrance, op.cit., (p. 23).
18. ibid, (p. 45).
19. ibid, (p. 31), "In the doctrine of the Church as the Body of Christ, everything turns upon the fact of the resurrection of Jesus Christ in body, and by his Ascension in the fulness of his humanity". Cf: S. G. Wilson, *The Gentiles and the Gentile Mission*, (1973 p. 105), "Thus while it (Ascension) marks a division between the story of Jesus and the history of the Church, much more significant is the way in which it firmly links these two epochs".
20. ibid, (p. 31).
21. Cullmann, op.cit., (p. 195).
22. Barth, op.cit., (p. 127), "Christ founds His Church by going to the Father, by making Himself known to His Apostles...here is the start of the mission, the sending of the Church into the world and for the world".
23. C. K. Barrett, Luke the historian in recent study, (A. S. Peake Memorial Lecture No. 6, 1960, p. 57f.).
24. Torrance, op.cit., (p. 85).
25. Haenchen, op.cit., (p. 183), "The Spirit bestowed on the Exalted was not

an endowment of which he had need: it was given him only for distribution!".

CHAPTER SIX

1. Davies, op.cit., (p. 41), "If, therefore, the Transfiguration was prefigurement of the Parousia, it must logically be a prefigurement of the Ascension too, and, as such it is presented in the third Gospel". For a full discussion on this latter point, see further the same author in 'The Pre-figurement of the Ascension in the Third Gospel', *J.T.S.* Vol. 6, (October 1955 p. 229f.).
2. Ramsey, *The Resurrection of Christ*, (1961, p. 23).
3. R. H. Fuller, *The Mission and Achievement of Jesus*, (1954, p. 84), "there is not a single passage whereby he directly claims to be Son of God...but he did know that he stood in a unique relationship of Sonship to God...not a dignity to be claimed, but a responsibility to be fulfilled".
4. Cf: "I do always those things which are pleasing to him (John 8:29); "My meat is to do the will of him that sent me and to finish his work" (John 4:34).
5. Fuller, op.cit., (p. 88f.), "We conclude that...this Sonship was to find the essential pattern of its obedience in the fulfilment of the destiny of the Isaianic Servant".
6. Cf: R. P. Martin, 'Carmen Christi, Philippians 2:5–11 in recent interpretation and in the setting of early Christian worship', *S.N.T.S.*, (1967, p. 231f.), "The transition from humiliation to exaltation is denoted by διό which prepares for what follows by introducing the result of His obedient submission unto death. The καί marks the element of reciprocity, the use of διὸ καί makes it clear that the best translation is 'that is why'...a vindication of all that the obedience involved".
7. Moule, 'St. Paul and Dualism, The Pauline Conception of Resurrection', *S.N.T.S.* Vol. 12, No. 2, (1966, p. 122).
8. ibid, (p. 107).
9. Cf: A. D. Martin, 'The Ascension of Christ', *The Expositor*, Vol. 16, (July-December, 1918, p. 344),

   "...that moment reached when the full glory of the Son of Man as a type of all our race, wrought out the final separation from earthly conditions, and Manhood stood revealed as accomplished in the Divine. All that truly belonged to our personal life reached its destiny, the end for which, through unnumbered ages the Spirit of God had worked at His chosen design. And though we exclude that vulgarizing of the event which would present it to us as a something staged, let us be careful to realise that the whole activity of the Lord was involved".

10. Moule, 'Expository Problems, The Ascension-Acts i.9' *Exp.T.* Vol. 68 No. 7, April, (1957, p. 208).
11. ibid.
12. Cf: Davies, *He Ascended into Heaven*, (1958, p. 182), "We may indeed see man's ultimate goal revealed and already attained by Jesus, who has trodden the whole path of human destiny". Cf: Torrance, op.cit. (p. 14), "...He has ascended, presenting Himself eternally before the face of the Father, and presenting us in Himself".
13. Cf: J. A. T. Robinson, *Twelve New Testament Studies*, (S.B.T., No. 34, 1962, p. 162), "Baptism affords...participation in the whole descent and ascent of Christ, which was enacted proleptically in the water-baptism of Jesus himself".

14. Flender, op.cit., (p. 19).
15. Cf: Barth, op.cit., (p. 125), "Christ is now, as the Bearer of humanity, as our Representative, in the place where God is and in the way in which God is. Our flesh, our human nature, is exalted in Him to God. The end of His work is that we are with Him above".
16. F. F. Bruce, 'Paul on Immortality', *S.J.T.*, Vol. 24, No. 4, (Nov. 1971, p. 469), "In some sense the spiritual body of the coming age is already being formed (Cf: 2 Cor. 4:16) so that physical death will mean no hiatus of disembodiment but the immediate enjoyment of being at home with the Lord (2 Cor. 5:8)". Cf: W. R. Matthews, *Some Christian Words*, (1956, p. 35f.), "It seems to me reasonable to believe that we are weaving our spiritual bodies as we go along. They are being formed by our thoughts and acts of will and imaginations during this life...we are to be preparing for that better body, the spiritual body, which God has for us". See also T. F. Glasson, *His Appearing and His Kingdom,* (1953, p. 108), "St. Paul's words about a 'spiritual body' are not a contradiction in terms but rather a useful way of combining the ideas of continuity and identity with that of a higher mode of existence".
17. Cullmann, op.cit., (p. 228), "The Holy Spirit who is indeed already at work, has not yet transformed earthly bodies into 'spiritual bodies'. That will happen only in the future (Romans 8:11, 23, 1 Cor. 15:35f)". See also 'Notes on Recent Exposition – A Controversial Study' – Professor Cullmann, *Immortality of the Soul or Resurrection of the Dead*? (Epworth Press, ET. 1958) *Exp.T.* Vol. 69, No. 10, (July 1958, p. 289f.). A thorough review is given in this assessment, and the theme of Cullmann can be summarized in one quotation, when the reviewer says, "Cullmann now asks, 'When does this transformation of the body take place?' 'The whole New Testament', he affirms, 'answers: At the End, and this is to be understood literally, that is in the temporal sense...the condition of the believing dead is one of 'sleep' until the Last Day'".
18. Cave, op.cit., (p. 291), Paul's "prime concern was to lead men to a communion with God in Christ which death, so far from terminating would not, as he later learnt, be able even to interrupt...the eternal life begun on earth shall reach in heaven its consummation".
19. Cf: 2 Peter 3:8, "But do not ignore this one fact, beloved, that with the Lord one day is as a thousand years, and a thousand years as one day".
20. Cf: Moule, The Birth of the New Testament, (1962, p. 98), "To each individual who responds there is already a coming of the Holy Spirit; already the disciple is where Christ is. But there is nothing here to replace the corporate consummation of the whole People of God as a future event". Again, "The visible resurrrection body of Jesus was the first-fruits and guarantee, not of escape from this world, but of its redemption, and they (i.e. Christians of the Apostolic Age) looked for a corporate event, still in the future – the raising of all God's people together in a new life, the emancipation of the body (not *from* the body), Romans 8:23. They affirmed corporate redemption as against individual escape". Ibid (p. 101).
21. Cf: R. P. Martin, op.cit., (p. 292f.), "...an increasing identification with His 'form' by the Spirit in this life, a process to be completed in the resurrection of the body, when Christians will take on the full shape of the glorified body of the risen Lord (2 Cor. 3:18, Romans 8:29, Phil. 3:21, 1 Cor. 15:49)".
22. Moule, 'St. Paul and Dualism The Pauline Conception of Resurrection', *S.N.T.S.* Vol. 12. No. 2, (1966, p. 116). Cf: L. Hodgson, *And was made Man*, (1928, p. 126),

"It is difficult enough to say what is the same in an acorn and the oak what it becomes; how can we then dogmatize about the principle of continuity between a physical and spiritual body? If we believe that after the death of our Lord Jesus Christ, there was such a continuity, we shall be wise to admit that we are ignorant of the 'mechanism' of the event which thus remains mysterious to us, a fact which we may symbolise by using to describe it the word of a foreign language, 'non reditus sed transitus'".

23. A. D. Martin, op.cit., (p. 340). Cf: C. S. C. Williams, 'The Nature of the Risen Body', in *Peake's Commentary on the Bible*, ed. M. Black and H. H. Rowley, 1962 edition, p. 964f.),

"The gist of the argument (i.e. 1 Cor. 15:42, 'it is raised in incorruption'), is that the actual physical particles of the earthly body are not raised up but that a spiritual body or expression of the man's whole self-continuous with his earthly body but different from it, will be provided for him on the heavenly plane... A Feuillet points out that the contrast in 2 Cor. 5:1–3 between the earthly and the heavenly tabernacle awaiting the Christian is paralleled here by contrast between the first and second Adam; the heavenly tabernacle he takes to be Christ's glorified body... without losing his identity, the risen Christian will be 'in Christ', as in a sense he is on earth already and will be part of the glorified body of Christ".

24. Cf: A. M. Ramsey, *The Resurrection of Christ*, (1961, p. 54), "Nor is it clear that what happens for 'mankind' in general must determine what should fittingly happen for Jesus Christ, for may not the Resurrection have been, not a typical survival to illustrate the fact that all good men survive, but a unique redemptive act whereby death was conquered for our sake?". And again, "Thus, if the evidence is pointing us towards a Resurrection of an utterly unique sort, we will not be incredulous, for the Christ is Himself a unique and transcendent fact in history". ibid (p. 57).
25. Cf: Davies, op.cit., (p. 66f.), "The Ascension is the means of opening to believers an entrance (εἴσοδος) into heaven, an entrance which Christ has renewed (ἐνεκαινίσεν) in so far as He has made available for others, the road by which He Himself travelled. He is therefore, in virtue of His Ascension, the forerunner of those who are to follow after". Cf: Ramsey, op.cit., (p. 56), "For the Gospel in the New Testament involves the freedom of the living God and an act of new creation which includes the bodily no less than the spiritual life of man". See also Moule, *The Significance of the Message of the Resurrection for Faith in Jesus Christ,* (S.B.T., Second Series No. 8, Second Impression 1970, p. 10) where he states that, since God never creates without a purpose, it is not inconceivable to regard "the total matter of this time-space existence...destined by the Creator not to be 'scrapped' but to be used up into some other existence".
26. L. S. Thornton, *The Common Life in the Body of Christ*, (1941, p. 285).
27. W. Bright, 'And, now, O Father, mindful of the love' in *The Baptist Hymn Book*, (1962), Hymn No. 307 verse 2.
28. Cf: Milligan, op.cit., (p. 26,)

"When, therefore, we speak of our Lord's Ascension into heaven, we have to think less of a transition from one locality than of a transition from one condition to another. *A change of locality is indeed implied* (italics mine), but it need not be to a circumscribed habitation like that of earth; it may be only to a boundless spiritual region above us and encompassing us on every side. The real meaning of the Ascension is that, in that closing act of His history upon earth our Lord withdrew from a world of limitations and darkness and sorrows to the higher existence where 'in the presence of God there is fulness of joy, and where at His right hand there are pleasures for evermore'".

29. Cf: Cullmann, op.cit., (p. 176f.), "Our final transformation at the end of the days (reception into the spiritual body) takes place through our adaption to the likeness of Christ, the Heavenly Man, Romans 8:29".
30. Moule, 'Expository Problems, The Ascension- Acts i.9', *Exp.T.* Vol. 68 No. 7, (April, 1957, p. 209).

CHAPTER SEVEN

1. Davies, op.cit., (p. 175).
2. Swete, *The Ascended Christ*, (1916, p. 128).
3. Cf: Argyle, *The Christ of the New Testament*, (1952, p. 167),

   > "In Paul's case, as his interest in the speedy Parousia of Christ declined, the 'Futurist eschatology' of his earlier phase falls into the background, and yields the foremost place to what has been called 'Christ mysticism', the assurance of present union with Christ as life-giving Spirit, Christ being in the Christian, and the Christian in Christ...this assurance of fellowship with the Exalted Christ, which is eternal life finds consummate expression in the Fourth Gospel. There eschatology is almost completely spiritualised; but not entirely. The futurist note is still occasionally struck (6:39–40, 44, 54, 5:25–29)...the eschatological theme in fact, runs right through the New Testament (cf 21:22)".

   Cf: J. Stewart, *A Man in Christ*, (1954, p. 200f.),

   > "Here Paul and the fourth evangelist join hands. The keynote of the Johannine literature is eternal life. This life resides in Jesus, who communicates it to men...but this does not rule out the conceptions of future resurrection and judgement and glory...the references to the future stand where they do, not in spite of the dominant idea of eternal life in the present, but just because that idea finds in them its complement and full significance. Both Paul and John were convinced that a life so glorious as that which in Christ they already enjoyed must one day, in the mercy of Providence, break its bands asunder and leap clear from all limiting conditions whatever, and be crowned by God in heaven".

   See also A. Richardson, op.cit., (p. 55f.), "At the 'apocalypse' of Christ in the 'last time' it will be impossible for anyone, with or without faith, to avoid beholding him as he is, in his glorious majesty". Cf: C. E. Raven 'The Message of Advent, *The Cambridge Review*, Vol. 74, No. 1801, (January, 1953, p. 235), "...if there are those who wilfully blind themselves to all care for God and neighbour, who become totally self-involved and incapable of penitence, then we may remember that Gehenna, the fire that is not quenched, is the rubbish-destroyer not the torture-chamber of the Holy City".
4. Swete, op.cit., (p. 130).
5. J. Dupont, 'The Conversion of Paul' from *Apostolic History and the Gospel*, (ed. W. Ward Gasque and R. P. Martin, 1970, p. 192).
6. Flender, op.cit., (p. 3f).
7. ibid, (p. 93).
8. ibid, (p. 94). As he says, "The exaltation of Christ and the renewal of the world eventually coincide". ibid, p. 106. See also R. P. Martin, op.cit., (p. 277f.).
9. Flender, op.cit., (p. 99).
10. ibid (p. 98). Cf: Kümmel, op.cit., (p. 121) where, referring to Acts 3:19–21 he writes, "It is...completely unfounded to interpret the speech of the taking up of Jesus into heaven (1:7–8) as an expression of the delay of the parousia (Bultmann, Haenchen, Grässer). The author saw as well as the eschatological consummation fulfilled in the present, beginning with the

sending and the exaltation of Jesus, as he expected its final fulfilment by the parousia of Jesus. This insight is confirmed by the connection which is established in 1:11 between the Ascension and the Parousia".

11. Cf: J. A. T. Robinson, 'Expository Problems, The Second Coming – Mark xiv.62' *Exp.T.* Vol. 67 No. 11, (August, 1956, p. 339), "His marked omission of the coming on the clouds, confining Jesus' prophecy simply to the session at God's right hand, merely reveals him as a consistent theologian, since for him Christ's enthronement did indeed take place from the Resurrection onwards, but His coming is reserved for the future". While this illustrates the point of the immediacy of the Reign of Christ, 'From now on (ἀπὸ τοῦ νῦν) the Son of Man shall be seated at the right hand of the power of God', we believe that the Reign begins at the Ascension, for Luke, rather than at the Resurrection, as earlier we have sought to demonstrate.
12. Flender, op.cit., (p. 101).
13. A. M. Ramsey, *The Glory of God and the Transfiguration of Christ*, (1949, p. 125),

    "Why has the Transfiguration this high importance, being cited even in preference to the Resurrection? (1) It was a proof of the coming Parousia of Jesus Christ. Those who witnessed it saw in anticipation 'the power and the coming of Jesus Christ'. (2) It bore witness to the prophetic word; it confirmed the truth of the whole body of prophetic teaching which spoke of the messianic age. This for 'Peter' is the supreme importance of the Transfiguration...it is like a lamp in a dark place, bringing the illumination of the Gospel until the light of the Parousia shines within the hearts of Christ's people".

14. Torrance, op.cit., (p. 59).
15. ibid (p. 58).
16. ibid.
17. Cf: J. Stewart, op.cit., (p. 261), "Although Christ is already present, His coming is still expected; although Christians are already redeemed, still must they await for the full redemption; sonship is theirs' now, and yet they still have to obtain it; they are already glorified and yet hope for glory; they possess life, but life they must yet receive. (J. Weiss, Das Urchristentum, 421)". See N. Perrin, *The Kingdom of God in the Teaching of Jesus*, (1963), for a comprehensive survey from Schleiermacher to present day theologians, and his comment concerning the ministry of Jesus when he says, "The important thing is that all of these (i.e. 'the consummation of all things', the coming of the kingdom 'in power', or the 'coming' or the 'day' of the Son of Man, or the term 'Kingdom of God') are different ways of expressing the same conviction, that what had begun in his ministry would necessarily issue in a final and perfect consummation; the Kingdom of God was both a present reality and a future hope" (p. 140).
18. Cf: Ramsey, op.cit., p. 83, "Our present discerning of the glory of God by faith is not worthy to be compared to the vision of Glory when we shall see Him as He is. In this glory, not only redeemed humanity, but all creation will share, though it groans now in bondage and awaits its deliverance into the liberty of the glory of God's children. Romans 8:18f."
19. Cullmann, op.cit., (p. 103f.).
20. Cf: J. B. Phillips, *Letters to the Young Churches*, (1947, p. 212f.), where he renders 1 John 3:2, "Here and now we *are* God's children. We don't know what we shall become in the future. We only know that, if reality were to break through, we should reflect His likeness, for we should see Him as He really is!".
21. H. Burnaby, *Thinking Through the Creed*, (1961, p. 52).

22. Swete, op.cit., (p. 136).
23. T. F. Glasson, *His Appearing and His Kingdom*, (1953, p. 191f.). Cf: Milligan, op.cit., (p. 57), "Neither at the Resurrection nor the Ascension was His work completed. It is going on now, and it will continue to go on until, so far at least as the present dispensation is concerned, it closes with His manifestation in the glory of the Father, and the kingdom of the earth becomes, not by right only, but in reality, His kingdom." See also E. Rust, *The Christian Understanding of History*, (1947, p. 294f.). Cf: A. M. Hunter, *Interpreting Paul's Gospel*, (1954, p. 128). See further C. F. D. Moule, *The Birth of the New Testament*, (1962, p. 103), "Apocalypse...is a way of conveying, in symbol and pictorially the conviction of the ultimate victory of God".
24. R. P. Martin, op.cit., (p. 268).
25. ibid (p. 270).
26. T. F. Glasson, *The Second Advent*, (1945, p. 137) where he says that the Anointing at Bethany, the Ethical Teaching of Jesus, the creation of the New Israel, and the sending of the Gospel to all Gentiles," show that Jesus did not expect the end of the world in the near future."
27. Barth, op.cit., (p. 128).
28. ibid.
29. Cf: Ramsey, op.cit., (p. 34), "So near was it that it was not so much a 'coming' as already a 'presence' of the Lord with His people, a *permanent* presence moreover, which not even absence from sight for a little while could really interrupt, and which, when fully established, would last forever. (Quoted from St. Paul's Epistles to the Thessalonians by George Milligan)". See also Torrance, 'Immortality and Light', *Religious Studies*, Volume 17 Number 2, (June 1981, p. 161), "...everything that the Christian Gospel tells us about the hope for personal, immortal life is bound up with the final Advent of Jesus Christ which must be given its full space-time reality as an event of basically the same nature as the resurrection of Jesus Christ from the grave. But what took place intensively there is Jerusalem will unfold in all its extensive reality, embracing the whole universe in a new heaven and a new earth. That is the divinely appointed destiny of the created universe, and it is within that destiny that each of us will enter upon the inheritance prepared for us, in Jesus Christ in God".

CHAPTER EIGHT

1. Cf: Davies, op.cit., (p. 170), "...the modern realization that the New Testament record was written in the light of the Resurrection requires modification in so far as it must be affirmed that these writers lived, not only in the days of the Resurrection, but also in the days of the Ascension. Nor is this mere tautology: the two are distinct, however intimately they be connected".
2. Argyle, 'The Ascension', *Exp.T.* Vol. 66 No. 8, (May 1955, p. 241).
3. van Stempvoort, op.cit., (p. 37), "Acts must follow Gospel...Luke was the first to begin the great task of writing that new history. That he has done it brilliantly may be seen in his second version of the Ascension in Acts."
4. Torrance, op.cit., (p. 58). Cf: Davies, op.cit., (p. 174), "By His withdrawal of Himself at the Ascension from the realm of the visible, Christ provides the occasion for faith, which is the bond of union with Him in His exalted state. *Now* is the time of faith, not of sight".
5. Conzelmann, op.cit., (p. 184), "Between Ascension and Pentecost, there is

an interval without the Spirit. Thus the Spirit enables us to see on the one hand, the individuality of Jesus, his position in the centre of redemptive history, and, on the other hand, the continuity between him and the Church, or in other words, the postive link with the present".

6. Barth, op.cit., (p. 125), "The Ascension...means, at any rate, that Jesus leaves earthly space, the space which is conceivable to us and which He has sought out for our sakes...since He stands *above* this space, He fulfils it and becomes present to it. (Cf: Eph 4:10)". Cf: Flender, (op.cit., p. 146), "The Exalted Christ can speak to our contemporary situation without becoming a transcendent figure out of touch with history altogether".
7. Moule, 'Expository Problems, The Ascension-Acts i.9' *Exp.T.* Vol. 68 No. 7, (April, 1957, p. 209).
8. Cf: Luke 24:39f, John 20:20, (cf: Matthew 28:9), John 21:12f, Acts 1:3f.
9. Barclay, *Crucified and Crowned*, (1963 Second Impression, p. 176).
10. Cf: Metzger, op.cit., (p. 84), "The Ascension of Jesus follows necessarily as part of the logic of his bodily resurrection". See also Conzelmann, (op.cit., p. 203), "There is...a state in which Jesus is risen and glorified, but not yet exalted". Cf: G. R. Beasley-Murray, *Christ is Alive*! (1947, p. 148), "The Ascension was an act calculated to show that His place was with the Father; that He was not only alive but the Lord exalted to the throne of God".
11. Cf: Psalm 118:22. See also F. F. Bruce, 'New Wine in Old Wine Skins 111 The Corner Stone', *Exp.T.* Vol. 84 No. 8, (May 1973, p. 231f.).
12. Cf: Romans 8:34, Sanday and Headlam, *The International Critical Commentary*, (1905, p. 221), "ὅς καί... it is not a dead Christ on whom we depend, but a living. It is not only a living Christ, but a Christ enthroned, a Christ in power. It is not only a Christ in power, but a Christ of ever-active sympathy, constantly (if we may so speak) at the Father's ear, and constantly pouring in intercessions for His struggling people on earth. A great text for the value and significance of the Ascension (Cf: Swete, *Apost. Creed*. p. 67f.)". Cf: A. Richardson, 'The Ascension', *Exp.T.* Vol. 79 No. 8. (May 1968 p. 249), "Until the final victory, the cross in the heart of God still remains. Our High Priest in the heavens is not untouched by our infirmities...all the sufferings of mankind, are more costly to God than they are to us. This is part of the meaning of the Ascension".
13. Torrance, op.cit., (p. 24), "The Spirit...comes from the Father in the Name of the Son...as 'formed Spirit' (filioque), the Spirit of Christ, so that the term 'quickening Spirit' (πνευμα ζωοποιουν) can be applied to Christ Himself as well as to the Spirit. (John 6:63, 1 Cor. 15:45, 11 Cor. 3:6, 1 Peter 3:18)".
14. ibid. (p. 45), "Christ had distanced His Body from us and yet through His Spirit He has come and filled the Church with His own Self".
15. Davies, op.cit., (p. 177).
16. Cf: Conzelmann, op.cit., (p. 206), "The next event after the Ascension in the series of mighty acts no longer affects the course of events in Jesus' life, and the Church only secondarily, but it affects the Church directly: the outpouring of the Spirit".
17. The Collect for Ascension Day in the *Book of Common Prayer*.
18. Davies, op.cit., (p. 180).
19. ibid (p. 182).
20. *A. Souter, A Pocket Lexicon to the Greek New Testament*, (1916, p. 252), "συντέλεια with αἰῶνος a characteristic expression of Jewish apocalyptic, *conclusion*, *consummation*, *end* of the present period of time".

21. Cf: G. H. Boobyer, *St. Mark and the Transfiguration Story*, (1942, p. 68),

"Now in heaven, Christ has a radiant δόξα form (2 Cor. 3:18, Phil. 3:21, etc.,), and at his coming upon clouds, he will appear in like manner (Phil. 3:20, Col. 3:4,2 Thes. 1:9, Titus 2:13, 1 Peter 4:13, 5:1). Christians at that day will be changed into the same kind of δόξα body to share his triumph with him (1 Cor. 15:43, 51–4, 2 Cor. 3:7–18, 4:17, Phil. 3:20f, Col. 3:4, 2 Thess. 2:14, 2 Tim. 2:10). In fact, when Christ's radiant δόξα appearance is mentioned by the New Testament, it is predominately around the thought of his shining form in heaven, or at his coming at the End that the minds of the writers revolve".

22. Swete, op.cit., (p. 157f.). Cf: A. M. Hunter, op.cit., (p. 127n,) "Jesus is gone up, and has sat down, and shall forever sit, on the throne of the universe. (Letters of Dr. John Brown, 86)".
23. Davies, op.cit., (p. 174).
24. Bultmann, op.cit., (p. 171). Cf: Flender, op.cit., (p. 164) who shows that Luke tackles the problem of the ongoing history of the world in which the Christ Event was staged, as it now relates to the new order which Christ brought in.
25. Cullmann, op.cit., (p. 225). As he observes, the verb καταργεὶν has two meanings (a) to subject, (b) to destroy. 2 Tim. 1:10 describes the victory over death already achieved, whereas 1 Cor. 15:26 uses it to describe victory only after the return of Christ at the end.
26. J. S. Stewart, *The Life and Teaching of Jesus Christ*, (Church of Scotland Publications Committee, Vol. 11, May, 1952, p. 208f.). See article in *Theology*, Vol. 76 No. 641, (November, 1973) by C. F. D. Moule on 'The Distinctiveness of Christ', (p. 562f.), passim.
27. R. P. C. Hanson, *II Corinthians*, (S.C.M. Torch Bible Commentary, 1954, p. 50), "The Incarnation meant that he was not only the Representative, but also the incorporated Head of the human race, not merely its leader or finest example, but the personified principle of its existence".
28. Moule, op.cit., (p. 572).
29. Cf: Conzelmann, op.cit., (p. 177f.), "Christ shares with God the title Lord, but at the same time, his subordinate position is maintained as a matter of principle (1 Cor. 15:28, cf: Phil. 2:6f)".
30. Barth, op.cit., (p. 126). Cf: Davies, op.cit., (p. 169), "The Ascension belongs not to the periphery, but to the heart and substance of the Gospel".
31. Cf: Moule, 'Expository Problems, The Ascension-Acts i.9', *Exp.T.*, Vol. 68 No. 7, (April, 1957, p. 209).
32. J. H. Bernard, 'Ascension and Assumption' in *Encyclopaedia of Religion and Ethics*, Vol. 2, (ed. J. Hastings, 1909, p. 157). Cf: Swete, *The Ascended Christ*, (1916, p. 154), where in asking as to the value of the Ascension today, he replies, "Can any subject which is so transcendent that it cannot be expressed in terms of human experience without calling in the aid of symbolism, be of practical value to our modern life?...circumstances have changed...and the present age needs to have its attention directed to matters of more immediate interest, such as the intellectual and social problems which beset us today, and clamour for a speedy solution". Such words indeed, have a modern ring about them, for what Swete wrote in 1916 could well have been written in 1983. But his answer lies in the seven sections, summarizing his book whereby he demonstrates the absolute relevance of the Ascension in any and every age, and its relation to the contemporary problems of life in every sphere. As we have attempted to show in this essay, the more Christ is exalted, the nearer he comes to us in daily living.

33. T. P. Ferris, *The Interpreter's Bible*, Vol. 9, (1954, p. 26). Cf: Swete, op.cit., (p. 164), "The doctrine of the Ascension and the Return, must be presented afresh to our generation, in the sterness of its imperious call to a recognition of the claims of Christ over the individual life".
34. C. S. Mann, 'The New Testament and the Lord's Ascension', *C.Q.R.*, 158 (1957, p. 465).
35. Cf: W. Barclay, op.cit., (p. 177f.), "As Denney finely says, the Ascension is the proof that manhood is destined for heaven and not for the grave, that manhood is destined, not for dissolution but for glory".

Bibliography

Argyle, A.W. *The Christ of the New Testament*, (1952).
——'The Ascension', *Exp.T.* Vol. 66 No. 8, (1955).
Bacon, B.W. 'The Ascension' in Luke and Acts, *Expositor* Vol. 7, (1909).
Barclay, W. *Crucified and Crowned*, (1961).
Barrett, C.K. *The Gospel according to St. John*, (1955).
——'John' in *Peake's Commentary on the Bible*, (ed M. Black and H.H. Rowley, 1962).
——*From First Adam to Last*, (1962).
——*Luke the historian in recent study*, (A.S. Peake Memorial lecture No. 6, 1960).
Barth, K. *Dogmatics in Outline*, (ET. 1966).
Beasley-Murray, G.R. *Christ is Alive*! (1947).
Benoit, P. *Jesus and the Gospel*, Vol. 1. (ET. 1973).
Bernard, J.H. 'Ascension and Assumption' in *Encyclopaedia of Religion and Ethics* Vol. 2, (1909).
Boobyer, G.H. *St. Mark and the Transfiguration Story*, (1942).
Book of Common Prayer. Collect for Ascension Day, (1662).
Bruce, F.F. 'The Ascension in the Fourth Gospel', *Exp.T.* Vol. 50 (1938/39).
——*Commentary on the Book of the Acts: The English Text with Introduction, Exposition, and Notes*, (1954).
——'New Wine in Old Wine Skins: III. The Corner Stone', *Exp.T.* Vol. 84 No. 8, (1973).
——'Paul on Immortality', *S.J.T.* Vol. 24, No. 4, (1971).
Bultmann, R. *Theology of the New Testament*, Vol. 1 (ET. 1952).
Burnaby, H. *Thinking Through the Creed*, (1961).
Burnaby, J. 'Review of J.G. Davies, *He Ascended into Heaven*', *Exp.T.* Vol. 70 No. 7, (1959).
Cave, S. *The Doctrines of the Christian Faith*, (1952).
Church Times 'True Record', (May 25th, 1973).
Clark, N. *Interpreting the Resurrection*, (1967).
Clarke, W.K. Lowther 'The Clouds of Heaven. An Eschatological Study', Theology, Vol. 31, 1935.
Conzelmann, H. *The Theology of St. Luke*, (ET. 1961).
——*An Outline of New Testament Theology*, (ET. 1968).
Creed, J.M. *The Gospel According to St. Luke*, (1930).

Cullmann, O. *The Christology of the New Testament*, (ET, 1959).
——'Immortality of the Soul or Resurrection of the Dead?' in Notes of Recent Exposition, *Exp.T.* Vol. 69 No. 10, (1958).
Davies, J.G. *He Ascended into Heaven*, (1958).
——'The Prefigurement of the Ascension in the Third Gospel', *J.T.S.*, Vol. 6, (1955).
Denney, J. 'Ascension' in *A Dictionary of the Bible*, (ed. J. Hastings, 1898).
Dewar, L. *The Holy Spirit and Modern Thought*, (1959).
Dibelius, M. *Studies in the Acts of the Apostles*, (ET. 1956).
Dodd, C.H. 'The Appearances of the Risen Christ: an Essay in Form-Criticism of the Gospels', *Studies in the Gospels*, (ed. D.E. Nineham, 1955).
——*The Founder of Christianity*, (1971).
——*The Interpretation of the Fourth Gospel*, (1953).
——'The Life and Teaching of Jesus Christ' *A Companion to the Bible*, (ed. T.W. Manson, 1945).
Dunn, J.D.G. 'Spirit and Kingdom', *Exp.T.* Vol. 82 No. 2, (1970).
Dupont, J. 'The Conversion of Paul' in *Apostolic History and the Gospel*, (ed. W. Ward Gasque and R.P. Martin, 1970).
Enslin, M.S. 'The Ascension Story', *J.B.L.*, Vol. 47, (1928).
Evans, C.F. *Resurrection and the New Testament*, (1970).
Farmer, W.R. 'The Last Twelve Verses of Mark', *S.N.T.S.*, (1974).
Flender, H. *St. Luke, Theologian of Redemptive History*, ET. 1967).
Flew, R.N. *Jesus and His Church: A Study in the Idea of the Ecclesia in the New Testament*, (1938).
Foakes-Jackson, F.J. *The Acts of the Apostles*, (Moffatt Commentary, 1931).
Fuller, D.P. *Easter Faith and History*, (1965).
Fuller, R.H. *The Foundations of New Testament Christology*, (1965).
——*The Mission and Achievement of Jesus*, (S.B.T., 1954).
Glasson, T.F. *The Second Advent*, (1945).
——*His Appearing and His Kingdom*, (1953).
Gundry, R.H. 'The Form, Meaning and Background of the Hymn Quoted in Timothy 3:16' *Apostolic History and the Gospel*, (ed. W. Ward Gasque and R.P. Martin, 1970).
Hanson, R.P.C. *II Corinthians*, (Torch Commentary, 1954).
Harnack, A. *The Acts of the Apostles*, (ET. 1909).
Harrison, P.N. *The Problem of the Pastoral Epistles*, (1921).
Haenchen, E. *The Acts of the Apostles*, (ET 1971).
Hodgson, L. *And Was Made Man*, (1928).
Hunter, A.M. *Interpreting Paul's Gospel*, (1954).
Jeremias, J. *The Eucharistic Words of Jesus*, (ET. 1955).
Kümmel, W.G. *Introduction to the New Testament*, (ET. 1965).
——'Promise and Fulfilment', *S.B.T.*, (ET. 1961).
Lampe, G.H.W. 'Luke' in *Peake's Commentary on the Bible*, (ed. M. Black and H.H. Rowley, 1962).
——'The Holy Spirit in the Writings of St. Luke', *Studies in the Gospels*, (ed. D.E. Nineham, 1955).
——and MacKinnon, D.M. *The Resurrection*, (1966).
Leaney, A.R.C. *The Gospel According to St. Luke*, (1958).
Macgregor, G.H.C. *The Growth of the Resurrection Faith*, 1, (1939).
——and Ferris T.P. 'St. Luke' and 'Acts' in Interpreter's Bible, Vol. 9, (1954).
Mann C.S. 'The New Testament and the Lord's Ascension', *C.Q.R.*, 158, (1957).
Martin, A.D. 'The Ascension of Christ', *Expositor*, Vol. 16, (1918).
Martin, R.P. *Carmen Christi*, (1967).

Matthews, W.R. *Some Christian Words*, (1956).
Metzger, B.M. 'The Ascension of Jesus Christ' in *Historical and Literary Studies, Pagan, Jewish and Christian*, (1968).
Milligan, W. *The Ascension and High Priesthood of our Lord*, (1892).
Mitton, C.L. *The Epistle to the Ephesians*, (1951).
Moule, C.F.D. *The Birth of the New Testament*, (1962).
——'The Distinctiveness of Christ' *Theology*, Vol. 76 No. 641, (1973).
——'Expository Problems, The Ascension-Acts i.9' *Exp.T.* Vol. 68 No. 7, (1957).
——'Further Reflections on Philippians 2:5–11' *Apostolic History and the Gospel*, (ed. W. Ward Gasque and R.P. Martin, 1970).
——*The Phenomenon of the New Testament*, (S.B.T., 1967).
——'St. Paul and Dualism, The Pauline Conception of Resurrection', *S.N.T.S.*, Vol. 12, No. 2, (1966).
——ed. *The Significance of the Message of the Resurrection for Faith in Jesus Christ*, (S.B.T., Second Series, No. 8, 1968).
Mowinckel, S. *He That Cometh*, (1956).
Packer, J.W. *The Acts of the Apostles*, (1966).
Perrin, N. *The Kingdom of God in the Teaching of Jesus*, (1963).
——'Mark 14:62: The End Product of a Christian Pesher Tradition?' S.N.T.S., Vol. 12, No. 2, (1966).
Phillips, J.B. *Letters to the Young Churches*, (1947).
Preston, R.H. and Hanson, A.T. *The Revelation of St. John the Divine*, (Torch, 1955).
Ramsey, A.M. 'Ascension' *A Theological Word Book of the Bible*, (ed. A. Richardson, 1951).
——*The Glory of God and the Transfiguration of Christ*, (1949).
——*The Resurrection of Christ*, (1945, 1961).
——'What was the Ascension?' *S.N.T.S.*, Bulletin II (1951).
Rashdall, H. *Philosophy and Religion*, (1909).
Raven, C.E. 'The Message of Advent', University Sermon in *The Cambridge Review*, Vol. 74 No. 1801, (1953).
Richardson, A. 'The Ascension', *Exp.T.*, Vol. 79 No. 8, (1968).
——*An Introduction to the Theology of the New Testament*, (1958).
Roberts, H. *Jesus and the Kingdom of God*, (1955).
Robinson, H.W. *The Christian Experience of the Holy Spirit*, (1952).
Robinson, J.A.T. *But that I can't believe*! (1967).
——'Expository Problems, The Second Coming – Mark xiv.62', *Exp.T.* Vol. 67, No. 11, (1956).
——*Twelve New Testament Studies*, (S.B.T., No. 34, 1962).
Ropes, J.H. *The Beginnings of Christianity, Part 1, Acts of the Apostles*, (1925).
Rust, E. *The Christian Understanding of History*, (1947).
Sanday, W. and A.C. Headlam 'The Epistle to the Romans' *The International Critical Commentary*, (1905).
Sasse, H. 'Jesus Christ the Lord, the Exalted' *Mysterium Christi*, (ed. G.K.A. Bell and A. Deissmann, 1930).
Schweizer, E. *Jesus*, (ET. 1971).
Scott, E.F. *The Epistle to the Ephesians*, (Moffatt Commentary, 1952).
Simon, U.E. *The Ascent to Heaven*, (1961).
Souter, A. *A Pocket Lexicon to the Greek New Testament*, (1916).
Stanton, V.H. *The Gospels as Historical Documents*, (1909).
Stauffer, E. *New Testament Theology*, (ET. 1955).
Stewart, J.S. *The Life and Teaching of Jesus Christ*, (Church of Scotland Publications Committee Vol. 11, 1952).

——*A Man in Christ,* (1954).
Streeter, B.H. *The Four Gospels,* (1927).
Swete, H.B. *The Apostles' Creed,* (1894).
——*The Appearances of Our Lord after the Passion,* (1915).
——*The Ascended Christ,* (1916).
Tait, A.J. *The Heavenly Session of Our Lord,* (1912).
Taylor, V. *The Person of Christ in New Testament Teaching,* (1958).
——'The Passion Narrative of St. Luke, A Critical and Historical Investigations', Ed. O.E. Evans *S.N.T.S.*, Vol. 19, (1972).
Thornton, L.S. *The Common Life in the Body of Christ,* (1941).
Tinsley, E.J. *The Gospel According to St. Luke,* (1965).
Torrance, T.F. 'Royal Priesthood', *S.J.T. Occasional Papers* No. 3, (1955).
——'Space, Time and Resurrection', 1976.
——'Immortality and Light' *Religious Studies* Vol. 17, No. 2, (1981).
Trudinger, L.P. 'ἁρπαγμός and the Christological Significance of the Ascension', *Exp.T.* Vol. 79 No. 9, (1968).
Turner, H.E.W. 'Expository Problems, The Resurrection', *Exp.T.* Vol. 68 No. 12, (1957).
van Stempvoort, P.A. 'The Interpretation of the Ascension in Luke and Acts', *S.N.T.S.*, Vol. 5, (1958–59).
Whitaker, D. 'What Happened to the Body of Jesus? A Speculation', *Exp.T.*, Vol. 81 No. 10, (1970).
Wilder, A.N. 'Ancient Traditions of the Resurrection in Acts' *J.B.L.*, Vol. 62, (1943).
Williams, C.S.C. *The Acts of the Apostles,* (1957).
——*Alterations to the Text of the Synoptic Gospels and Acts,* (1951).
——'I Corinthians' in *Peake's Commentary on the Bible,* (ed. M. Black and H. H. Rowley, 1962).
Wilson, S.G. *The Gentiles and the Gentile Mission,* (1973).